BASIC CHRISTIANITY

MARGARET ERB

InterVarsity Press
Downers Grove
Illinois 60515

Contents

© 1952
by Inter-Varsity
Christian Fellowship.
All rights reserved.
No part of this book
may be reproduced
in any form without
written permission
from InterVarsity Press.

Eighth printing,
April 1974

Library of Congress Catalog
Card Number: 67-28874
ISBN 0-87784-401-1

Printed in the United
States of America

one

INTRODUCTION TO "BASIC CHRISTIANITY"

WHAT IT IS

Basic Christianity is a study of some basic doctrines of the Christian faith. Its scope is somewhat limited, since only eight short passages of Scripture are used. *The aim* in writing this series has been to give the student a thorough understanding of eight Scripture passages so that he may be able to turn to them and explain to another person God's plan for man's salvation.

Because Basic Christianity contains only eight studies, many aspects of the Gospel have not been touched upon. While it is doctrinal in nature, every effort has been made to keep it relevant to contemporary student life. The series can readily be covered in one school term, and perhaps what is lacking in it can be made up through succeeding Bible studies.

HOW TO USE IT

IT'S FOR THE LEADER

Basic Christianity is a Bible study guide for the *leader* of a Bible

3

study group. The equipment for other students is simply the open Bible, a notebook and a pen.

THE LEADER MUST STUDY

If you were to look up the word "study" in a dictionary you would find that among other things it means *"the application of the mind to books."* In the case of Bible study it is the application of the mind to the Book of books. Of course, Bible study involves other things too, like the application of the will and of the life to the Book, and reliance upon the Holy Spirit as the Teacher. But just as these are essential to successful Bible study, so is hard work. If you do not wish to spend a lot of time studying the Bible and preparing to lead a Bible study group, it would be better if you did not attempt this series of studies. Most of them are quite lengthy and detailed, and the bulk of the material will tend to confuse rather than help the person who has only a half-hour in which to prepare a Bible study.

But if you are willing to take time and to rely upon the Holy Spirit for His teaching, you will find BASIC CHRISTIANITY a definite help in your Bible study group.

MEMORIZE

If BASIC CHRISTIANITY is to be of value after it has been studied the leader should urge the students in the group to memorize where to find the eight passages of Scripture used, i.e., Psalm 139, Romans 1, John 8, John 3, John 1, Hebrews 7, Colossians 2 and Acts 1. Then when a student has interested a friend in the Gospel he can explain the Way, using some or all of these passages as a basis for his instruction.

BREAK IT UP IF NECESSARY

Each chapter is designed for a good forty-five to sixty minute Bible study, although a few chapters can be handled in half-hour periods.

Your immediate reaction to the studies may be that you can't possibly cover all that territory in one session. However, if you study them carefully you will find that each study has one or perhaps two main points. If you head for those main points and do not allow too much irrelevant discussion to cloud the issue you can do the studies in the allotted time.

If you do not have enough time in your group to go through a whole study in one session, you may divide it into two. The longest studies are marked where it is suggested that you break them into two sections. Or rather than break up the study you may wish to go completely through the whole passage at the first session, not stopping long for discussion. Then in the second session go over the main ideas and discuss them.

NUMBERING

The leader should note that the leader's study questions do not correspond with the numbering of the group study. The leader's questions are designed to help the leader get for himself the main theme or themes of the passage. Unless he has thought through the passage and it has become real to him he cannot teach it well. The group questions have the same purpose, but there are some extra questions that are used as interest-catchers or to illuminate certain points.

ITALICS

Don't let the italics confuse you. Usually they are for summary purposes rather than for emphasis. When you have finished your studying you will probably want to jot down the main questions you want to ask the group and then leave BASIC CHRISTIANITY at home. However, if you do teach directly from it the italicized parts should bring to your mind the sequence of thought as you glance down the page. The way it is italicized is not the way that will be most helpful to everyone, so if you don't like it, do your own. BASIC CHRISTIANITY is a guide; avoid following it slavishly.

ABBREVIATIONS

RSV—Revised Standard Version of the New Testament, revised 1946

ASV—American Standard Version of the Bible, revised 1901

EVALUATE

The detail with which BASIC CHRISTIANITY has been written is largely for the purpose of helping you with your *method* of leading a Bible study. It should be a help with other studies, not just this series. When you have led a study that went well, sit down for a few minutes afterward and try to figure out and write down the reasons for its success. Do the same if things seemed to go flat. By doing this faithfully you should be able to improve your teaching technique considerably over a period of time.

MEET THE GROUP'S NEEDS

Remember that *you are dealing with people*. The need of your group on a certain day may not be met by the particular theme stressed in the study for the day. Don't try to achieve the aim for the day at the expense of meeting your group's needs.

two

WHAT IS GOD LIKE?

a leader's guide for group study of Psalms 139:1-6

STUDY FIRST

"I certainly got a lot out of that study you led today." If you want the students to say that about the Bible study you lead, *DON'T* read the rest of this chapter until you have done the following assignment.

A. Get the impact of the passage as a whole by reading Psalm 139 with your thoughts focused on what you are reading.

B. Study vv. 1-6 in detail and answer these questions as *fully* as you can, writing down the answers.

    1. What persons are mentioned in vv. 1-6?

    2. What relationship exists between these persons in vv. 1-5? (When one person makes contact with another, one of them has to make the first move. For example, "A man that hath friends must show himself friendly." Who is taking the first step in contacting the other party in this Psalm?)

    3. List, in your own words, everything that God knows about "me" in vv. 2-4.

4. What three areas of "my" life are dealt with here? See especially vv. 2b, 3b and 4.

5. Write down your reactions to the fact that God is thoroughly aware of these three areas of your life.

6. What does v. 5 add to the picture of God? List everything you would know about Him if this were the only information you had?

7. In your life, where have you seen God's hand laid upon you? How did you react to that hand?

8. How did the author of this Psalm react to the kind of God described in vv. 1-5? If you are stuck, look at vv. 6, 7, 14 and 23, 24.

C. Spend a few minutes thinking about the one or two main points of this study which have spoken to you.

BE PREPARED

Here are a few things which will add a lot to the effectiveness of your study if they are attended to ahead of time.

1. A week ahead of time, ask someone who reads well to prepare to read this Psalm intelligently to the group. Ask the reader to locate a copy of the ASV so that the Psalm may be read in more modern English than the King James. Most people mentally close their eyes and go to sleep when the Scripture is being read in our churches. This is because they are so familiar with the Bible and it is usually very poorly read. Whenever Scripture is read aloud in your meetings try to have the reader prepared ahead of time so that he can read so that it will have meaning for those who listen.

2. Announce ahead of time that for this series of studies the students should bring a Bible, notebook and pen. Notes on little scraps of paper are readily lost. Encourage each person to keep a regular notebook for the Bible study notes.

HAVE AN AIM

"He who aims nowhere gets there." Your aims for today should be as follows:

1. Initially, to capture the group's interest in the series of studies on Christian doctrine upon which you are embarking.

2. To show clearly to each person that

a. God is not far off and totally indifferent to the life of the average young person, but rather *He is fully aware* of every fellow's and girl's thoughts, actions and words.

b. *God is in touch* with each life, and has laid His hand upon it in an effort to bring it into a happy relationship with Himself.

HAVE A METHOD OF PROCEDURE

Introduce the study quickly. The first study should begin with some introductory remarks which will serve to whet the group's appetite for the Word which you are studying today and during succeeding weeks. You might begin something like this:

"*Suppose one of your friends were to say to you,* 'I don't believe much in God. I guess there is such a person, but I don't think He cares very much about humans.' Or perhaps, 'You Christians are too narrow minded; I believe that anyone who is sincere in his religion will get along O.K.' If that happened *would you be able to take that friend and sit down with the Bible and study with him* the passages upon which you base your beliefs?

"*One of the commands in the Bible says that we are to study* to show ourselves approved unto God; we are to be workmen who don't need to be ashamed of our work because we can rightly divide the Word of truth. Peter says that we should be ready at any time to give a quiet and reverent answer to anyone who wants a reason for the hope that we have within us (II Timothy 2:15; I Peter 3:15). *Could you give a reason from the Bible for the various things you believe?* Well, we are starting a series of studies today which should help us to have some of the answers.

"Now, the *logical place to start a study* of the basic doctrines of the Christian faith *is with the character of God* because He is the Author of true religion.

"*Some people think of God* as a benevolent old man. Others, as a bright fiery force that started the world in **motion and then left** it to run itself. Others say God is Mind or Intelligence. What does the Christian say God is like? *Here is what several Christians said:* 'God is a person, a loving heavenly Father who looks after His children. He is also the ruler of the universe,' 'God is like Christ. He is not an abstract, far-off Spirit,' and 'God is merciful and just.' Well, it's a big subject and we certainly won't ever exhaust it. But *by the end of our study today you'll know where to find and how to explain one passage* dealing with the question, WHAT IS GOD LIKE?"

This sounds long for you to remember. Don't try to remember it all, and whatever you do, *don't* read it off to the group. Just digest **some** of the ideas (the key thoughts are italicized) and put a few of them into your own words. All you want to do is to get the students interested in what we're studying before we start the actual study rather than jumping right into it by saying, "Today we are studying Psalm 139 about the character of God."

Don't spend longer than five minutes on your introduction.

You know, I think leading a Bible study when you want the whole group to take part is one of the most difficult things to do. It is far easier to stand up and give a little sermon or even to have the group open their Bibles and follow along while *you tell them* what you got out of it. But to lead the group while they study all together and *find out truths for themselves* is quite another matter! If you've tried it once you know what I mean. And I'm sure you will forgive me for writing in such a detailed way as if you were five-year-olds. I thought I would write it exactly as I would teach it, for the first few studies at least, and then if you have never done this sort of thing before you will know exactly what to do. But please do not feel bound to follow it slavishly. It is a *guide*, not a formula to be followed step by step in every detail. The words in quotes are what I would say if I were leading your Bible study. In general the italics are for summary purposes rather than for emphasis. It is done so that you can run your eye quickly down the page as you are leading the study and the italicized parts will bring to your mind the main questions you want to ask the group, and the main content of the page.

CONCENTRATE ON THE MAIN BODY OF TRUTH

1. (Familiarize the group with the passage.) *Ask the Holy Spirit,* who is the Author of the book you are studying today, to explain it to you all.

a. *Have the passage read aloud* to the group by the reader you chose while the students listen with their Bibles closed. Ask the group to notice what God is like while he reads. When the reader is finished have the group jot down *from memory* what they learned about God. Give them two minutes to do this.

b. *Ask someone for one thing he noticed.* Ask someone else for another until you have all the findings of the group. (You will probably get some answers like this: God knows everything about me; God is everywhere; God punishes evil; God leads people, etc. Thank each person who offers an answer; and when you have all the answers try to repeat them quickly to the whole group so that the group gets a summary of all the answers.)

"Each of these characteristics of God that has been mentioned is important, and we could spend an hour studying each one. But today we are going to concentrate on those mentioned in the first six verses. *Will you open your Bibles to Psalm 139, please?"*

2. *Find out who are mentioned in the passage, and what is said about them.*

    a. *Ask the group what persons are mentioned in vv. 1-6.* (Do not wait long for obvious answers any time you are leading a study. If someone does not answer quickly, then ask a specific person for the answer. When a question is difficult, it is better not to embarrass people, especially newcomers or younger ones, by asking them the answer unless you are quite sure they either know the answer or won't mind saying so if they don't. But when the question is an easy one, don't be afraid to call people by name and ask for answers. Try to get the students, in answering any question, to state, first of all, exactly what the Bible says. It is all right later on to explain what the words mean, but first of all see what it says. For example, vv. 1-6 are talking about "God" and "me." Commend the person who answers this way, rather than the one who says the passage is about "God and someone else" or "David" or "the author.")

> "It is interesting that this passage is about 'God' and 'me,' for after all the person each of us is most interested in is 'myself.' Now let's see what's going on between God and me."

    b. *Have the group list briefly everything mentioned about God in vv. 1-6.* Have them state each fact in a complete sentence. For example, in v. 1, "God has searched me," "God has known me." This listing should be done very quickly. Anyone who can read can answer this question, so do not be afraid to have each person state one thing about God. Have them begin at v. 1 and go right through to v. 6.

3. *Find out what relationship exists between the persons in this passage.* Have the group state one thing that is common to all the facts listed about God. If no one gets the idea, point out that

in each case God is the subject, and man the object. All religions are concerned with the question of the relationship between God and man. In most other religions we find man seeking after God. Do we have a God who sits away off and lets man look for Him, or does our God make the first move and seek after man? Wait for someone to answer this question, and ask him to illustrate his answer to this question; then ask him to illustrate his answer from this passage. If he cannot do so, point out that God is the active one, and man the passive. It is *God who searches*, knows, compasses, is acquainted with, and lays His hand upon man. It is *man who is searched*, is known, etc. Here then we have the first great fact about God. He takes the first step toward man; it is God who seeks to establish a relationship with man, not man who searches for God.

4. *Find out what it is that God knows about me.*

"Will you please study verses 2-4 carefully. See if you can *find three specific aspects of every person's life* about which God knows."

The answer you want here is "thoughts," "actions," and "words." If the group suggests other things like "my downsitting" and "my path," you might reply, "Yes, that's right, but it is not one of these three definite aspects of life that I want us to see." If they need some help, ask them to look at vv. 2b, 3b and 4.

"Now let us think about each of these things a little bit: thoughts, actions and words."

5. *Discuss Thoughts*

a. "Look at the phrase, 'understanding my thoughts afar off.' *Is there any difference between being known and being understood?* What is it?"

Try to get the group to see that "understanding" has in it the idea of "knowing" *plus* "being in sympathy with that which is known."

God does not just "know" our thoughts, but He understands them; He knows why we think the things we do. He understands the things that your friends and parents don't understand, no matter how much you tell them. He knows why you are discouraged sometimes, and why your hopes rise high at others.

> **b.** *"Now consider the words, 'afar off.' What do you think they mean?"* Someone may suggest that it *means my far away thought*, or *my daydreams.*

Discuss whether daydreams have any value at all; whether it helps to know that God understands your dreams about the future, your hopes, your ideals, your fears, the things you wouldn't dare put into words to a friend because the friend might take it as a joke when you're not joking. Surely it does help to know that God understands them.

Another person may say that "afar off" *means that God is far away, and yet He understands our thoughts.* You might point out that this shows another wonderful characteristic of God: He is not just the far-away God, the ruler of the universe, but He is also near to each one of us, and can read our thoughts like an open book. *Ask the group to think for one minute which of their thoughts they would not like God to understand.* What should be done with these thoughts (see Psalm 51:10)?

A third suggestion may be that *God knows our thoughts while they are still afar off*, i.e., *before they are yet really complete thoughts,* while they are just very vague ideas. Point out that this too shows God's wonderful insight into man's mind. Do not dwell long on each of the suggestions made, for we still have a lot of ground to cover. Summarize the section on thoughts something like this:

> *"God thoroughly understands all of our thoughts. Therefore we should bring them all to Him, the far off ones, asking Him to help us accomplish our high*

goals; and the unkind and mean ones, asking Him to help us think more about others. We must come daily and hourly to the One who understands all our thoughts, and ask Him to purify and cleanse and improve our thinking habits, for 'as a man thinketh in his heart so is he.'"

6. *Discuss Actions*

What words in vv. 2-4 have to do with actions? The group should list the following: downsitting, uprising, path, lying down, ways. Have the group quickly state these in their own words. Keep asking them for ideas until they have suggested something like this: God knows every time I sit down or stand up. He sees me wherever I go during the day, and knows when I retire at night; in fact, He is thoroughly acquainted with all of my actions.

"Now let us consider for a moment that one phrase, 'Thou compassest my path and my lying down.' What does this mean?"

Point out that we could interpret this verse to mean that my path (my activities during the day) and my lying down (my sleeping hours) are *all within the circle of God's observation.*

"How would you feel if all your activities—those done outside and those within the four walls of your room— were written on the blackboard for all to see? How do you feel when you know your life is as plain to God as the writing on a blackboard? Are you afraid of Him or do you want to ask Him to remove the wrong things and make your life the way He wants it to be?"

Do not have the group answer these questions aloud. Just let them think their answers, as you pause a bit between each one.

7. *Discuss Words*

"Now let us go to 'words' in v. 4. *What does the word 'altogether' add to this verse?*"

Someone may suggest that it means *all kinds of words*. Ask him then *what kinds of words we use*. Point out, for example, that there are encouraging words. Get the group to list others such as, foolish words, complimentary words, happy words, loving words, lying words, gossipy words, etc. God knows them "altogether."

Another may say the "altogether" means that God knows not only the exact words, but the *meaning in the words*. He knows the thoughts that prompt them, the meaning of the tone in your voice. Our words often conceal our real thoughts. How often we reply to thanks by saying, "You're welcome," when what we have done has been done in a grudging spirit. God knows your words *altogether*.

8. *Summarize*

"Here, then, we have a great God who is thoroughly and intimately acquainted with *me*, and *my* thoughts, *my* actions, and *my* words."

9. *Find out if man has any contact with this God who knows so much about him.*

"We are now coming to a very important point in our study. People may say to you, 'Yes, I know God knows everything about me. He knows *everything*. But so what? He's up in heaven, and I'm down here, and I have no contact with Him, nor He with me.' This is the idea many heathen religions give of God. God is all-knowing, but He is also far away, so it doesn't matter too much. But the Christian religion is different. *What does v. 5 add to our description of God that is important for us to know?*"

If the group does not get the idea that God has put Himself into personal contact with every man, ask them to state v. 5 in their own words. When they say, "God is in front of me, and behind me, and His hand is on my shoulder," they will get the point that *God is in touch with men.*

10. *Find out how men respond to God who knows men, and touches men.*

a. *"How do you react when someone puts his hand on your shoulder?"*

Help the group to see that if it is a person you like, you will stay and enjoy the security and the bond of friendship which that touch symbolizes. But if it is a person whom you don't like, or whom you have wronged, you react quite differently. You try to wriggle loose from the hand, and get away from the person.

b. *"Have you felt God's hand upon your life? How has He touched you? How did you react to that touch?"*

Each of these is a personal question. The students may not want to answer them aloud, but encourage a few to give one or two illustrations or explanations of how God has touched them, and how they responded to that touch. Tell the group anything you can from your own experience.

c. *"How did the author of this Psalm react to God?"*

Let the group think for awhile and then draw their attention to the following verses if they have not already mentioned them: vv. 6, 7, 14, 23 and 24. Point out that the author was amazed and praised God. But he also thought of trying to run away from God. Then he realized that this couldn't be done. Instead he decided to stay under God's touch, and be led by God into the "way everlasting."

CONCLUDE QUICKLY

Never leave the study up in the air at the end. Always bring it to a definite conclusion.

> "*Eternal happiness is found only in God,* and in living in His presence. *We can try to wriggle out* from under the hand of God who knows all about us, or *we can stay* and ask Him to search our hearts, to remove the evil that is there, and to lead us in a happy, useful life in fellowship with Himself."

Have each person answer to himself these questions: *How do you react* to this kind of God who knows all about you, and who has laid His hand upon you? *Do you feel uncomfortable* in His presence? *Do you like to stay near Him,* and enjoy His presence? You do not want anyone who has been touched by God's Spirit to leave the group today with a question in his mind as to how he can come into that fellowship with God which we have mentioned. Therefore you might say something like the following in closing.

> "Some of us may be wondering how we can get to the place where we don't mind if God knows all about us, and where we want to stay in His presence. We may be wondering how we can come into fellowship with God. The Bible teaches clearly that we can come to God only through Jesus Christ who through His death paid the penalty for our sins. Since the penalty for sin has been paid, God is able to forgive us *all* of our sins, even though He *knows* so much about us. We must believe on Christ for the forgiveness of our sins. This subject—how a person can become a true follower of God—will be dealt with quite fully in some of the studies that follow, but if any of you want to find out more about it right away, you might start reading the Gospel of John in the New Testament, and you will find definite help there."

Close with prayer. Possibly use, from memory, the words of Psalm 139:23, 24.

Note: If you want to study other aspects of God's character, Psalm 103 will be useful.

three

WHAT IS SIN?

a leader's guide for group study of Romans 1:18-32

STUDY FIRST
Someone has said, "Success is one-tenth inspiration and nine-tenths perspiration." That is very true when it comes to Bible study. The following assignment probably won't make you perspire, but it will make you think if you do it properly.

1. What is sin? Try to write a definition.
2. List all the sins you can of which man is guilty.
3. Read through Romans 1:18-32 thoughtfully, referring to a dictionary in the case of any words which you do not understand, and writing the definitions down. Note the paragraph divisions (vv. 18-23; 24, 25; 26, 27; 28-32) which divide the passage into thought-units. Compare the list of sins in the passage, especially those in vv. 28-32, with the one you wrote.
4. Why do men commit all these sins? Is there anything basically wrong with man that makes him act this way? Find your answer in the text.

5. What do you think "God gave them up" means? Why did God give man up to sin (vv. 23-25)?

6. What is wrong with idolatry? What produces idolatry, according to the text? What forms of idolatry do you see among your friends and associates?

7. Study vv. 18-23 carefully. Who merit God's wrath? Why? Why is man without excuse? What does man know about God? Answer all these questions in your own words, making sure that you understand each word you use. For instance, it says they knew God's Godhead (v. 20). What does this mean? Note any words which may be translated differently, and more clearly, in the margin of your Bible. Read this passage in a modern translation if you have one (possibly the Revised Standard Version) because the King James translation in this section is quite difficult.

8. Write out a clear definition of sin, based on your study of this passage.

HAVE AN AIM

Most people have a distorted and confused idea of what sin is. For many Christian young people, the first thing that comes to their minds when sin is mentioned is "worldliness." To non-Christians, sin is usually gross crime, like theft or murder. They do not consider law-abiding citizens as sinners.

Your job today is to get the group really to think about the problem so that they come to an understanding of what sin basically is. If your conception of sin is dancing, smoking, etc., you have but a slim chance of winning your friend to Christ, for what you call sin is as normal a part of his life as eating and sleeping. He must be shown a deeper sin in his life if he is to feel his need of a Saviour. There are in every person's life *sins* such as are listed in vv. 28-32, but *from what do these sins come forth?* That is the question which should be clearly answered for all those in your study group today.

There are various ways the answer can be put. You have already written your definition. Others are given below:

> Sin is saying to God, "No! Let ME."
>> Sin is living as if God didn't exist
> Completely ignoring Him.
>> Sin is living independently of God,
> Running your own life.
>> Sin is refusing to let God interfere in your affairs.

HAVE A METHOD OF PROCEDURE

Introduce today's study quickly, and get the group interested in it. Here are some suggestions for doing this:

1. *Get the general setting by studying Romans 1:28-32 briefly.*

   a. *Ask each person to describe on paper the most detestable sinner he can imagine,* listing all the possible sins of which he could be guilty. (Allow three minutes to do this.)

   b. Have two people read their lists of sins, and then ask individuals in the group to add anything which was left out. *Have these sins listed on the blackboard.* (Do not let the group get into a discussion about whether a certain action is or is not a sin.)

   c. Next ask the group to listen while you *read the list of sins given in Romans* 1:28-32. Have someone write them on the board while you read. *Ask the group to compare the two lists.* Ask them what is included in the Bible's list that is not in the group's. Are they surprised? Why?

If no one has noticed that whisperers (those who speak in secret) are put on a par with murderers, and that the proud and disobedient to parents are listed along with the deceitful and God-haters, call their attention to the fact. Also have them note that other specific sins are mentioned in the two preceding paragraphs (vv. 24, 25; and vv. 26, 27). You can see that God calls some things sin which we do not. We call them little personality traits, or failures, but not sins that are worthy of God's wrath.

2. *Introduce the main question*: *What is behind all the sins of vv. 28-32?*

a. Now try to get the group to look for the cause behind all this sinning. What makes people do these sins? Is there some basic sin behind it all? In order to start the group thinking, you might use some ideas such as the following:

"You may often have heard the words quoted, 'All have sinned and come short of the glory of God' and 'The soul that sinneth, it shall die.' Perhaps you are trying to persuade a friend of yours that he is a sinner, and needs Jesus as his Saviour. And yet you do it with some misgiving because his life seems in many ways to be about as good as your own, and maybe better! For example, he is more conscientious about doing his school work, and more ready to help the other fellow out when someone around school needs help. But you know that anyone who has not trusted Christ as his Saviour is a sinner, and so you try to convince him of his need. However, he just can't see that he is a sinner, and you are at a loss to explain to him in what respect he is.

"The Bible says that Adam and Eve sinned, and that therefore all men are born sinners. *Have you ever wondered just what sin it is that we are born with? Maybe if we could get a better understanding of what sin actually is, we would be able to witness to our friends better.*"

(What you have done so far is simply an introduction to the main lesson. It can be done in about 8 or 10 minutes, so keep things moving. Don't waste a lot of precious time on it.)

CONCENTRATE ON THE MAIN BODY OF TRUTH

1. *Define sin*

   a. *Have each person write down a definition of what sin is.*

   b. *Have a few of the answers read aloud.* Commend those who have written it in their own words. Almost always when we express an idea in our own words we have a better understanding of it than when we use the Bible's or another's phraseology. By the end of our study today we hope the group will be able to give a Biblical definition of sin, and then they can compare it with the ones they have just written.

2. *Study vv. 22-28 to find out what sin actually is.*

   a. Have the group note vv. 24, 26 and 28 where it says "God gave them up" or what is perhaps nearer to the original Greek, "God delivered man over."

   b. *Ask them why God did this,* looking for an answer in the text. *If they do not get the answer* after a time, give them some such help as the following:

   > "Note in v. 24 the word 'wherefore.' If you were reading a school newspaper and your eyes caught the sentence, 'Therefore he was expelled,' you would look back to the previous sentence to see what the cause was. We often forget that the English in the Bible is governed by the same laws of grammar as modern English writing. Look at your Bible now. What does the 'wherefore' in v. 24 refer to in vv. 22, 23? What is 'this cause' of v. 26? What is the reason in v. 28 for God's giving them up?"

   c. *Note that the sin of idolatry is mentioned in both vv. 23, and 25. Ask them what idolatry is, and what is wrong with it.* If there is no satisfactory answer to the latter question, drop the question and tell the group you'll come back to it later. If the idea is suggested that idolatry is wrong because it is worshipping yourself rather than God, commend the answer and don't pursue the matter.

3. *Summarize briefly what has been done so far.*

   a. Man commits all kinds of sins (vv. 28-32).

   b. God lets man do this (vv. 24a, 26a, 28b).

   c. God has delivered man over to this kind of life because man worshipped things that he himself made, instead of worshipping God (vv. 23, 25, 28a).

> "That third point is beginning to get at what sin actually is. Let us spend the rest of our time studying vv. 18-22, and particularly v.21, to see if we can get a good understanding of what is wrong with idolatry, and what man's basic sin against God is."

The study can be broken into two parts at this point.

4. *List the five facts of v. 21.*

   a. *Have the group look first at v. 21. Ask what the five facts listed here about men are.* Question them until the following facts are listed:

> They knew God
> They glorified Him not as God
> They were not thankful to God
> They became vain in their imagination
> Their foolish hearts were darkened

Studying these facts is the most important part of today's study.

5. *Discuss the first fact: "They knew God."*

   a. "If you were surrounded by lots of things a certain person had made, you could tell quite a bit about that person's character, even though you had never met him. For example: If you were living in a house that someone else had built and completely furnished, *what might you be able to tell about that person?*"

Quiz the group until you get several suggestions. Some of the following might be suggested: his ability as a craftsman would be seen in the way he had built the house, his wealth would be seen in the materials he had used, and in the furnishings; his honesty would be seen in the thoroughness of the construction, etc.

> **b.** "When you look at creation, *what are the main things you can tell about the Builder? What does the author say you can tell about Him from the things He has made* (v. 20)?"

Ask where they can see evidence of God's *power* in creation (atom, universe, etc.). Where can they see evidence of His *Godhead*, of His being divine, superhuman (design in nature, regularity of the seasons, mechanics of the human body, etc.)? Everything that man knows must have a maker, and that this complete universe should have come into being by chance is an assumption which many excellent scientists of our day doubt. For some of them, the invisible things of God are clearly seen from the creation of the world (Cf. v. 20).

6. *Discuss the second fact: "They glorified Him not as God."*

a. *Ask what man's response to this knowledge was.* Have several state the fact "they glorified Him not as God" in their own words. Have them look at v. 28, which states a similar fact. The Revised Standard Version translates, "They did not like to retain God in their knowledge" as *"They did not see fit to acknowledge God."*

b. Have them try to think of a *present-day illustration* that would clarify the latter phrase. The *resistance movements in any satellite country* are one good example. "It may be the government in authority, but it's not going to govern us!" This attitude may evidence itself in several ways. The rebels may try to *ignore the new government,* and run their own affairs without any reference to it. Or they may acquiesce on the surface and rebel underneath, i.e., *they may go through the forms of swearing allegiance, etc., but not really mean what they say.* Have the group speculate as to any other way the patriots might show how they feel about the government. It will likely be suggested that they may break out into *open hostility,* and try to fight the new rule. All three types of rebellion are equally offensive to the new rule.

c. Try very carefully now to get the group to *apply this illustration* to our relationship with God. This is getting at the very heart of what sin is, and it is most important that we have the group thinking with us.

Ask someone to describe the person who is openly hostile in his relationship with God.

Ask someone else to describe the one *who ignores the new government.*

Have a third person describe the one *who has an outer shell of conformity but who really does not mean it.*

Ask which kind we usually think of as being a sinner? Are the other two sinners also? Make sure that some of the following ideas are brought out:

> "*The one in open hostility may be an atheist,* and proud of it; he may be one who openly fights Christianity; or he may be a drunk, a murderer, thief, sex pervert, etc. Whichever he is, 'nice people' would all agree that he is a sinner, and justly deserves the wrath of God.

> "*The one who ignores God* is not so readily recognized as a sinner, although 'church-goers' would likely be ready to classify him as such. He may be a perfectly law-abiding citizen, a doctor or a farmer or maybe a student. He ignores God, just lives as if God didn't exist. There are a great many of this type of sinner in our country, and their number is increasing rapidly.

BASIC CHRISTIANITY

"Then there is the third group. These people are hardly ever recognized as being among those 'who do not see fit to retain God in their knowledge.' *They are religious people.* They go to church at least at Christmas and Easter, if not every Sunday. Some of them say grace at meals. Some of them may go to the young people's meetings in their church, and the IVCF or ISCF meetings in their school. But they do not really love God; *they do not want Him to run their lives.* They are happy to sing, 'Holy, Holy, Holy, Lord God Almighty,' but they don't really mean it. They don't really want God to be the Almighty in their lives."

Summarize briefly here: All three groups may be very different in the outworking of their attitude toward God, but basically they are all the same. *They want to live independently of God and run their own lives. They do not honor God as God.* This is their basic sin against the God who loves them, and who created them.

7. *Discuss the third fact: "They were not thankful to God."*

a. Now finish up quickly the last three facts stated in v. 21. *Ask the group what saying "thank you" to a person shows about one's relationship to that person.* It will likely be stated that it shows one is indebted to the other person. But people often say, "thank you" without really *being thankful.* When men are thankful to God, they realize that they are indebted to Him for life and health, food and clothing, and for all that makes life worth living.

8. *Discuss briefly the fourth and fifth facts, "They became vain in their imaginations" and "their foolish hearts were darkened."*

a. Because the time is probably just about up, and we have covered the most important part of our study, I would suggest that you quickly go over this section, not asking many questions, but giving the information yourself. However, if you still have lots of time, or if you are taking this study in two periods, you can turn

28

your ideas into questions, and have the group discover for themselves what you want to put across.

b. It should be brought out that these last two facts are the result of not honoring God *as* God. *Somebody must be god in every person's life,* and for most people that somebody is themselves, until they ask God's forgiveness, and let Him become their God. "They became vain in their imaginations," simply means that they set their own intellects, their own ideals and thoughts on a pedestal and followed their own inclinations. Their foolish hearts, or, "senseless mind" as the RSV has it, are darkened so that *they cannot distinguish clearly the right and wrong of moral issues. They have a false set of values.* They set their faith on things that are not safe (like banks and insurance plans), and look for their happiness in things that do not satisfy (like popularity, power, travel, etc.).

9. *Define sin again according to their understanding of it from today's study, and illustrate the definition to make it clear.*

a. Ask them each *to write a definition of sin in their own words from what they have learned today.*

b. Ask them *why idolatry is so offensive to God, and whether worshipping images of wood or stone is the only kind of idolatry.* God hates idolatry because it is setting up your own standards of worship and religion instead of accepting God's and it is depriving God of the honor due Him. It can be seen not only in Africa and China, but in Canada or the U.S. When a man makes his money, his home, his brains, his friends, or his love for a good time the only thing that really matters to him, he is idolatrous.

c. Ask them *why rejecting Christ is the greatest sin* a man can commit. The idea should again be brought out that it is setting our minds above God's. It is saying, "I don't need the salvation you have provided. I will work out my own religion." Those who reject Christ reject God's best gift to mankind, God's only provision for man's sin (Cf. John 3:18).

10. *Note verse* 18.

a. In closing, go back to v. 18. *What is God's attitude toward sin?* All who have not had that sin forgiven are still recipients of that wrath, a wrath which no man can allay in his own strength.

b. If anyone wants to know today how sin can be dealt with in his or her life, take him to revelant Bible passages and show him. You might use John 3 in explaining that God's Son, Jesus Christ, bore God's wrath and took the punishment for us, when He was lifted up on the cross (Cf. John 3:14, 15). We must simply accept God's provision and believe in Christ for the salvation of our souls (Cf. John 3:16). However, if no one asks about it, you might simply mention that several studies will be spent on this subject, and that you will be dealing with God's answer to the problem of man's sin in the near future.

CONCLUDE QUICKLY

In concluding, I would simply read slowly and thoughtfully the following verses which have been chosen from today's passage. They are taken from the RSV and were selected because they bring out clearly the main ideas we have discussed today.

> "The wrath of God is revealed from heaven against all ungodliness and wickedness of men . . . What can be known about God is plain to them . . . His eternal power and deity have been clearly perceived in the things that have been made. So they are without excuse; for although they knew God they did not honor him as God . . . And since they did not see fit to acknowledge God, God gave them up to a base mind and to improper conduct" (vv. 18-21, 28).

I would then read Romans 3:21-25, which gives the cure for sin.

Note: If you wish to study any other passages on sin, you may refer to Romans 3:9-20; Isaiah 53:4-6; Genesis 6:5; Mark 7:1-23.

four

WHAT DOES SIN DO TO A PERSON?

a leaders's guide for group study of John 8:31-36

STUDY FIRST

1. So that you will have a good understanding of this passage use John 8:31-59 for your own study even though the group study should concentrate mainly on John 8:31-36. As you do so, try to imagine you have never read it before, and that you happened upon the scene in the Temple or on a street in Jerusalem. What emotions would you have seen on the faces of the people present?

2. To whom was Jesus speaking? Do not answer this question too quickly. Read completely through the passage before deciding. To which section of the crowd do you think Jesus was speaking in v. 34?

3. Upon what three things is freedom based, according to vv. 31, 32? Who must be Lord in one's life if one is to be free? Give Scripture references for your answer (Cf. also Romans 1:21).

4. If possible, look up in a concordance or a modern translation a more accurate translation of the word "servant" in v. 34.

5. Did the people to whom Jesus was talking realize that they were in bondage? To what were they enslaved? In what specific ways do you think they were enslaved? (You may have to use your imagination and knowledge of other Scriptures, although the passage itself gives some clues.) Why could the Jews not see their slavery?

6. Now apply this passage to the situation you are living in today.

a. Which of the people you know are included in the "whosoever" of v. 34? Do they know they are enslaved? Describe the kind of person who knows he is enslaved. How does he know it?

b. Do you have any friends whose conduct is in accord with Christian standards but who are not Christians? (For example, someone who has been reared in a Christian home who has not yet accepted Christ?) Do such people commit sin? If so, *in what way are they slaves?*

c. What types of slavery do you know of in real life? Think about these for a brief time. Do any of them help you to understand the spiritual slavery where the slaves do not know they are bound?

BE PREPARED
Ask someone from the group ahead of time to prepare to read the parts of the passage (vv. 31-59) which are spoken by the Jews. You then read Jesus' words. Leave out the introductory phrases such as "They answered him" and "Jesus answered them."

HAVE AN AIM
When asked what slavery to sin is, most people think immediately of excessive sins like chronic alcoholism or of gross crimes like theft and murder. Your aim for today should be to help the group to come to a better understanding of how *all* sin (petty or gross) *enslaves* people in that it keeps them from living the rich, full,

abundant life that could be theirs in Christ. Their eyes are blinded, and they cannot see that sin is *fencing them in* and *depriving* them of the privileges and opportunities of the Christian life. Yet they cannot break down the fence.

HAVE A METHOD OF PROCEDURE

Today's study requires a somewhat different method of approach than the two previous studies. Toward the end of the period you will probably have to do a little more talking than hitherto, because the idea that you are trying to put across today is foreign to the thinking of many Christian young people, and it may take them a while to understand it. However, the first part of the study will be just as usual with the leader asking questions and the group hunting for the answers in the text.

Introduce the study quickly. Your goal in the introduction today should be to have the group recapture the scene so that they get the full impact of the angry, threatening crowd, and Jesus' message of freedom to them. You might introduce the study somewhat as follows:

> "If you were trying to show a friend the importance of accepting Christ as Saviour, a logical place to begin is with his *need* of a Saviour. Supposing you have gone through Romans 1 with him. You have shown him that all men are sinners in refusing to let God run their lives, and that God's wrath rests upon all sinners. He might then say that he isn't much concerned about what happens in the next life. He might wonder if there were any *advantages in this life* in accepting Christ, or if it matters very much if he continues living as a sinner. We are going on from that point today to study the question, *'What does sin do to a person? Will it make any difference in my life if I continue to sin?'*

"The people in the Bible are real people. Sometimes we might be startled to find out just how real they are if we let them walk out of the Bible pages into our lives. Today the people we're about to study are having a conversation. *Let's pretend for a few minutes that we have never heard this conversation before,* and that we just happen to walk by as it is going on."

1. Have the group listen with Bible closed while you and the person you have chosen read the dialog. *Get the group's reaction to the conversation.* If they had overheard this on the street or in the halls of their school, what would they have done? Question the group until they see that this is an exceedingly tense moment. Anger and threats of murder are in the air!

2. *Ask them what the Jews are so disturbed about.* If they do not get it, call their attention to vv. 33 and 44. Is the Jews' statement in v. 33 correct? Why not? (Cf. the Assyrian and Babylonian captivities in II Kings 17, especially v. 23b, and II Kings 25: 21b.) However, they thought they were right for another reason. Can the group suggest what that might be? Someone will probably suggest that they were God's chosen people. He had delivered them from their enemies many times, and they were His special favorites! To be called children of the devil was insulting in the extreme.

3. You might ask the students to *imagine they are going to paint a picture* of the scene, and ask them what emotions they would express on the faces of those present. Do not leave this section until the students have a clear mental picture of the angry crowd, the sneering and rebellious faces, the loving Christ who is trying to make them see their need.

4. Give them time to read through John 8:31-36 silently before you begin the main part of the study.

BASIC CHRISTIANITY
CONCENTRATE ON THE MAIN BODY OF TRUTH

1. *Gather from the group the main facts of vv. 31-36.*

   a. Ask them *to whom Jesus was speaking in this passage.* To which section of the crowd do they think He was speaking in **v. 34?** If they do not get this, ask them if He was speaking of the Jews who had believed on Him (v. 31), or the Jews who were the devil's children (v. 44). It is quite likely that there were some Pharisees in the group since the attitude of some of those present is a typical pharisaical attitude. (Cf. John 7:45 ff., John 8:3, and John 8:13.)

   b. *Upon what three things is freedom based,* according to vv. 31 and 32? *Who must be Lord of one's life if he is to be free?* Have them give references for their answer (vv. 31, 47). Call their attention also to the passage we studied last week (Romans 1:21).

   c. Have the group *summarize the facts that are given in this passage regarding freedom and slavery.* Point out that the word "servant" in v. 34 is more correctly translated "slave." Three facts will emerge: the truth makes one free, committing sin enslaves one, the Son makes one free.

2. *Discuss the meaning of these facts for the Jews.* Our main concern today is to get an understanding of the second fact, "committing sin enslaves one." Jesus says, "Whosoever committeth sin is the servant of sin." The RSV puts it, "Every one who commits sin is a slave to sin."

   a. Ask the group *whether the people to whom Jesus was talking realized they were enslaved. To what were they enslaved? In what specific ways does the group think they were enslaved?* (As was mentioned in the leader's assignment, knowledge of other Scriptures and imagination will have to be used to some extent in answering this question. However, try to get some ideas from the group before you help them.)

BASIC CHRISTIANITY

"The Pharisees were self-righteous people. They thought they were much holier than other people, and they were critical of all who did not belong to their sect. They were *slaves of pride and slaves of criticism.* They could not enjoy other people because they had to criticize them. In other words, they were slaves of a *judging spirit.* Many fellows and girls are enslaved that way. They can't see the good in people.

"Most of the Jews were slaves in another sense as well. *They were living outside of the Canaan that God had intended for them.* God had promised them a land of their own, peace, prosperity, and a wonderfully happy relationship with Himself. But they were living outside of all this. They were under Roman rule. They were still longing for the Messiah and had no peace in their hearts because they were not living in fellowship with God.

"Jesus says (v. 34), 'Everyone who commits sin is a slave to sin' (RSV). The Pharisees were 'good living,' very religious people. But they were sinners. They had stopped following God, and were *following their own religion* (v. 37). The religious habits and practices which they had added to God's revealed law had become more important to them than God's first and most important command: 'Thou shalt have no other gods before me' (Exodus 20:3). They had stopped honoring God *as God* (Romans 1:21), and therefore they were not living the full and happy life God had intended for them."

b. *Why could they not see their slavery?* If the group cannot give any suggestions, have them note in v. 44 that Satan is a deceiver. It says elsewhere in the Bible that Satan has blinded men's eyes lest they should see the light of the Gospel and believe (II Corinthians 4:4).

The study can be broken into two parts at this point.

3. *Discuss the meaning of these facts for us today.*

   a. *Ask the group what people they know who are included in the "whosoever" of v. 34. Do they know they are enslaved?* There will likely be a difference of opinion here, which is as it should be.

   b. *Have them describe the kind of person who knows he is enslaved. How does he know it?* The person who knows he is enslaved is usually bound by some very bad habits which he knows he cannot break.

   c. "Now let us think for a moment about those people whose conduct is in accord with Christian standards but who are not Christians. Do such people commit sin? According to v. 34 are they slaves of sin? *In what sense are they slaves?*"

This last question is the key question of the study. You may need to enlarge upon the problem or just restate it so they see clearly what it is.

   "Most people, in our country at least, are like the Pharisees and *do not know they are enslaved to sin.*

   "The question is: *in what way are they enslaved?* If they are not gross sinners how can they be shown their bondage? Perhaps the answer for this question can best be deduced from a discussion of the kinds of slavery we know in the physical life."

4. *Compare spiritual slavery with physical slavery.*

   a. Discuss with them whether the slaves in a society which condoned slavery would always be unhappy. Would they all want their freedom? Would any of them not want to be free? It will likely be brought out that some of the slaves would be woefully ill-treated and really long for freedom while others would be treated kindly. The latter would love their master and be quite happy in their master's service. Would they have any desire to be emancipated? Some of them would prefer slavery because they would eat better food, and be better looked after than would be the case if they were freed. Others would crave their freedom even though it might mean greater physical hardship. *Freedom would mean new opportunities for them.* On the other hand continuance in slavery would mean *never being able to share in the privileges, opportunities and responsibilities of the free man.* There is no future for the slave.

> "Slavery to sin for many people in our land is much like the type of slavery just mentioned. The slave is not too unhappy, but he is not as happy as he would be if he were a *free servant of Christ!* Obtaining one's freedom *may* involve the giving up of some material advantages, perhaps a slight lowering of the slave's scale of living; but for the man who has really caught a glimpse of what freedom in Christ means, the loss of material possessions is insignificant when compared to the true riches of peace of mind and soul satisfaction which are gained. 'For a man's life does not consist in the abundance of his possessions' (RSV *Luke* 12:15).

> *"Man can never attain the wonderful destiny for which God intended him as long as he is a slave to sin. When he is freed life has a future, and living becomes purposeful!"*

b. *Roman Slavery.* Call the group's attention to another aspect of slavery.

"Many of the Roman slaves held positions of very high authority. Some of them were business managers in charge of all affairs of a large household. Others were well educated and were responsible for the complete education of the master's children. In most ways they enjoyed as much privilege and responsibility as the sons of the household. But there was one difference. *They were not heirs.* As long as they remained slaves they could be sold and bought at a moment's notice. They had no assurance of a permanent place in the household; and they had no rights as heirs of any property or assets if their master were to die. This is the point Jesus makes in v. 35. *The servant does not abide in the house forever;* he is not a permanent member of the household and he is not an heir. God had promised the Israelites an everlasting inheritance but they had become slaves to sin and were no longer heirs of God's promises.

"Similarly, those who have not been made children of God through Christ are not heirs of the Father and *will never share in the eternal glorious life which could be theirs"* (Romans 8:16, 17).

c. *A third kind of slavery.*

"There is another type of slavery: a bondage to poverty and ignorance. Many are thus enslaved, but are not aware of their condition of servitude. Only enlightenment as to the condition of others brings realization of their own slavery. Until such enlightenment comes, these people will deny that they are slaves.

"Do you not think that living in sin for many people is much the same type of bondage? Many of our friends may not be bound by perceptible chains of bad habits and vicious sins; but, *unless they are Christians they all are slaves of spiritual ignorance and poverty. Satan has blinded their eyes and like the man in ignorance who has never known anything other than a hard life, they do not know that there is an abundant life in Christ."*

5. *Contrast the slave's existence with the free man's life. Have the group draw up a list contrasting the life of a young person who is a slave to sin with that of one who is sharing Christ's abundant life.* They will have to do some real thinking in order to do this because many fellows and girls think of "giving up" things for Christ more than they think of accepting rich gifts from Him. Below are a few contrasts. The group will be able to think of others.

SLAVE TO SIN

Lack of purpose or meaning in life. "Life does not make sense." No assurance of being able to achieve. "A twist of fate" and the work of years may be worthless. He cannot count on luck being with him in the future.

His main satisfactions in life are found in money or the things money can buy in popularity in "having a good time." These do not satisfy the basic spiritual hunger which every man has. And often his pleasure is spoiled by the fear that they may be taken away from him at a moment's notice.

Feels misunderstood and sometimes unwanted in his home or among his friends and has to bear this alone.

Has a certain idea as to how he wants to behave and is frustrated in inability to live up to that ideal. Often finds he can't trust himself.

Is insecure in not knowing what is right and what is wrong and in not knowing what should be his standard of conduct.

FREE SON OF GOD

Life has meaning and purpose. Even though wars or other things may seem to thwart his plans he knows that God has a plan and purpose for his life.

Because God is guiding his life and working out a plan he need not fret when things seem to go wrong. His security is in God, not in circumstances.

His main satisfactions in life are found in fellowship with God, and in the deep joy and peace of mind which result from that fellowship. This basic hunger having been satisfied, he is able to enjoy all other aspects of life more completely. He does not have the same fear of losing his money, etc., since he knows that his main happiness in life is based upon God who can never be taken away from him.

Often has the same problems in being misunderstood, etc. as the other man, but has a God who thoroughly knows and understands him, and who can show him the way out of his difficulties.

Receives inner strength and power from God to live up to some of his ideals, at least, if not all of them.

Has the objective Word of God as well as personal guidance from God in matters of conduct and ethics.

CONCLUDE QUICKLY

1. "We have covered a lot of territory today, and because many of the ideas are new to you, you may feel somewhat confused. Let us summarize the most important facts of our study.

   "All who commit sin are slaves of sin whether they know it or not.

   "Many people do not know it.

   "The latter are deceived by Satan into thinking they are living quite a happy, adequate life, when in reality they are poor, wretched, miserable, blind and naked.

"The Son of God could set them free from this slavery, give them a rich, full, happy, useful life in this world and make them heirs of all the riches of God in an eternal life to come."

2. Have the group think for a moment what their responsibility should be to those who are slaves of sin. After they have made their suggestions, see that the following two points are brought out:

a. "None of us can convince a man of sin, nor of his slavery to it, nor of his need of Christ. It is the Holy Spirit who convinces of sin (John 16:8, margin). Therefore, it is our responsibility to pray for the Holy Spirit to open the eyes of our friends so that they may recognize their bondage.

b. "The Holy Spirit uses humans as instruments. Our lives should be so happy, purposeful and complete in Christ that our friends will see the lack in their own, will see the blessings which Satan is trying to keep from their sight, and will seek those blessings in Christ. A Christlike Christian is one of the best testimonies to the truth of the Good News."

Note: If you wish to spend another session on the subject of slavery to sin you will find Romans 6, especially vv. 12-23, helpful.

five

THE SOURCE OF NEW LIFE

a leader's guide for group study of John 3:1-16

STUDY FIRST

1. John 3:1-16 is an old familiar story—so familiar, in fact, that you may be thinking, "I wish I didn't have to study it again. I'd like something new." Therefore, do not begin your study today without first sincerely *praying to God for His guidance* and help, that this passage may once more have something fresh in it for you.

2. *Study John 2:23-25 carefully.* Decide what the following phrases mean: "believe in his name," "commit himself unto them," "knew all men." Write this paragraph in your own words. After you have studied the remaining questions on John 3:1-16, decide whether chapter 2:23-25 has any connection with chapter 3. If so, what is the connection?

3. What kind of person was Nicodemus? What do the words "Pharisee" (v. 1), "ruler of the Jews" (v. 1), and "master of Israel" (v. 10) add to the picture of Nicodemus? Look up these words in a Bible dictionary if you have access to one, or look up "Pharisee"

in an ordinary dictionary or encyclopedia. What possible reasons could Nicodemus have had for coming at night?

4. What are Nicodemus' opening words? Judging only by these, what do you think he had on his mind that he wanted to discuss with Jesus? In v. 3 it says, "Jesus answered him." Had Nicodemus asked a question? Do you think you could put what he was thinking in the form of a question? What is the connection between Jesus' reply and Nicodemus' opening remark?

5. State Nicodemus' next question in one word. Why did he ask it? What kind of kingdom were the Jews expecting? Is there any relation between the Jewish hope and Nicodemus' question about a literal human rebirth?

6. What verses do you think are included in Jesus' reply? (Since punctuation was lacking in the original manuscripts and the copies we possess, the quotation marks in the RSV are not necessarily correct.)

   a. What do you think "born of water" (v. 5) means? If you have access to a church library or a minister's library, look it up in a commentary.

   b. What two kingdoms does Jesus speak of in v. 6? How does one become a member of each kingdom?

   c. In v. 7 Jesus says, "Marvel not." Why?

   d. Write a short paragraph on the point of the illustration in v. 8.

7. Is Nicodemus satisfied by Jesus' answer? *State his next question in one word.*

8. *Study Jesus' reply in vv.* 10-13. What did Jesus expect Nicodemus to do even though he did not understand all about how the new birth takes place?

9. *What was Jesus' authority* for the emphatic statements He makes in vv. 3, 5, 7? (Cf. vv. 11-13.)

10. *To what incident does Jesus refer in v. 14a?* (Cf. Num.

21:4-9.) What was the people's sin? What was the remedy? What was God's part in it? What was the people's part in it? Was this the only remedy?

11. *To what incident does Jesus refer in v. 14b?* What is man's sin that made this remedy necessary? (Cf. Romans 1:18-32.) Is this the only remedy for sin? What was God's part in providing a cure for sin? What was Christ's part? What is our part in being cured?

12. Write down several illustrations that would help you to explain to a friend the difference between "knowing" that Jesus died for your sin, and "believing" that Jesus died for your sin.

13. *Meditate for five minutes* on the "so loved" of v. 16. What did it mean to God to give Jesus? What does it mean to God when you reject Jesus? If you have not been "born again" what ought you to do? If you have, what ought you to do?

14. *Prepare to read this passage aloud* to the group with all the meaning and understanding you can put into it. Pretend you are Nicodemus, and you just can't understand how the new birth takes place. Put true questioning expression into your reading of his questions.

15. *Pray for wisdom and power* to lead a good Bible study so that each person present will receive a message direct from God today. Please note that this is a very long study. It would be much better to cover it in two sessions than to hurry through it and have some people miss the point of the passage.

HAVE AN AIM

Aim to make it crystal clear to every person present that there are two kingdoms of which every man can be a member. *There is the fleshly kingdom,* the kingdom of man. *There is the spiritual kingdom,* the kingdom of God. In order to enter the kingdom of man, a person *must* be born into it. *In order to enter the kingdom of God, a person must be born into it.*

HAVE A METHOD OF PROCEDURE

Introduce the study quickly. Try especially hard today to gain the group's interest from the very outset because the passage is so very familiar to most of them that they will tend to be disinterested. I would start something like this:

> "When you were five years old you probably were very familiar with Humpty-Dumpty and The Three Bears. They were 'old stuff' to you. If you were brought up in a Christian home, or attended Sunday school regularly, you probably were just as familiar with Psalm 23 and the Lord's prayer. You could quote them long before you had much idea of what they meant. But there is a vital and inherent difference between the story of The Three Bears, or any other literature for that matter, and the Shepherd's Psalm. The former is a tale that is loved and appreciated at the age of three or four, but its appeal is very quickly outgrown. *The latter is the living Word of the living God. It never grows old.* You may be five years old, or you may be ninety-five, but as long as you are a sheep in the Good Shepherd's flock, the Shepherd's Psalm will be an inspiration and help to you.

> *"Today we are going to study one of those old familiar bits of Scripture, John 3:1-16. I wonder why it is so well known.* I wonder why John 3:16 is one of the first verses a child learns. What is the cardinal truth in the story surrounding that verse that makes it one of the best known facts about Christ. We shall study it today to see if we can get a better understanding of its message and a deeper appreciation for the God who made this story possible.

"Will you please *leave your Bibles closed and just listen while I read* this passage aloud? Listen to it as if you have never heard it before, and when I am through, be prepared to give me one new thing that you have never noticed before, or tell me the words which you think are the most important in the passage."

CONCENTRATE ON THE MAIN BODY OF TRUTH

1. *Familiarize the group with the passage. Read the passage aloud* to the group. *Ask the group for their findings.* (Don't spend a long time over this.) Just get one point from each person. Do not embarrass anyone. If a newcomer has nothing to say just say "OK," and go on to the next person with a smile. People do not usually mind taking part in a group study like this if the leader treats the whole affair in a casual manner, and does not act as if he pigeonholes as non-Christians all the people who can't answer a question.

When you have finished getting the group's findings, have them open their Bibles and study the passage together for the remainder of the time.

(Please note: If you have only a half-hour for this study and want to do the whole thing at one meeting, leave out the following section No. 2.)

2. *Study the context briefly.* Ask the group to read John 2: 23-25 to get the context of the story in chapter 3. Find out what kind of belief they think the "many" of v. 23 had, what it means for Jesus to "not commit himself to them," and the connection between this paragraph and chapter 3. When you have finished getting their opinions, tell them what conclusions you arrived at during your study of this section.

"Some people feel that Nicodemus' belief in Jesus was

rather a superficial one, and that he is an example of the people spoken of in 2:24, 25. He is the kind to whom Jesus would not 'open up,' and reveal the hidden things concerning Himself. Others, however, believe that the story of Nicodemus follows on 2:23-25 as a contrast. I am inclined to agree with them. This is a very intimate talk. Jesus does 'open up' to Nicodemus and confide in him some of the most precious truths about Himself and His mission that we have. For that reason, I think Nicodemus must have been a sincere seeker, and Jesus felt free to 'commit himself' to him."

3. *Get a picture of Nicodemus.* Now go on to chapter 3:1-16. Help them to *picture what Nicodemus was like.*

a. Ask *what a Pharisee is* (v. 1), what it meant to be a "ruler of the Jews" (v. 1), what it meant to be a "master of Israel" (v. 10).
Add anything that you found in your own study after the group has contributed all they can. Ask them to picture what it was like for a Pharisee, such an outstanding man, to come and visit Jesus of Nazareth. It was an unconventional happening. It is interesting that Jesus did not bow humbly to the dignitary and thank him for his opening remark. Instead, He spoke in accordance with His position as the Son of God; He went right to the heart of Nicodemus' trouble with no palaver.

b. Get their idea as to *why Nicodemus came at night.* Someone will be sure to suggest that he was ashamed of Jesus, and didn't want his fellow-Pharisees to see him visiting the Teacher from Nazareth. Ask them if there could be any other reason. If you don't get any suggestions and you have no others to offer, bring out the possibility that Nicodemus was busy all day, and came in the evening after work. Or maybe Jesus was busy all day and Nicodemus did not wish to take Him away from the crowds for a private interview. Or perhaps this was the only time in the day when Jesus was free to sit down and talk for a while. It is always so easy for us to assign wrong motives to people's actions. We should rather be ready to give them the benefit of the doubt. There is no indication in John 7:50-52 or 19:39 (the only other places where Nicodemus is mentioned) that Nicodemus was ashamed of Jesus.

4. *Discuss the opening remarks (vv. 2 and 3).*

a. Have someone state Nicodemus' opening words. If they were to judge only by this, *what do they think Nicodemus had on his mind?* Jews of the day were looking for the Messiah, and for the kingdom of God which the Messiah would usher in.

b. Point out that in v. 3 it says Jesus *answered* him. Had Nicodemus asked a question? *What relation is there between Nicodemus' remarks and Jesus' answer?*
There certainly must have been some question troubling Nicodemus or he would never have taken the trouble to come to Jesus. His opening remark could indicate that his thinking was running along this line: "I know you are a teacher come from God, but are you *the* teacher, are you the Messiah? Will you bring in the kingdom of God for which we have waited so long?" Nicodemus was knocking on the door of the kingdom without realizing it and Jesus told him how to enter.

5. *Discuss Nicodemus' first question (v. 4).* Have someone *state Nicodemus' question in one word.* Why did he ask it? What kind of kingdom were the Jews expecting? Is there any connection between the Jewish hope and Nicodemus' question about a literal human rebirth?
It will be brought out here that Nicodemus just couldn't understand how a *man* could be born again. He was thinking of a literal kingdom on earth, and physical birth as a Jew was the only requisite for entering it, in his opinion.

6. *Study Jesus' reply (vv. 5-8).* Ask *how many verses Jesus' reply includes.* Now have the group think through the ideas in Jesus' answer.

   a. Call their attention to v. 5 where Jesus says it is necessary to be born of water and of the Spirit in order to enter the kingdom of God. Have them give suggestions as to *what it means to be "born of water."*

Do not let the group get into a useless discussion here regarding baptism. Baptism is not the point we are studying today. Accept each suggestion and then summarize.

The term "water" is interpreted in various ways, and sometimes causes difficulty. The interpretation which seems most logical to me, especially in light of the context, is that water refers to the amniotic fluid in which a child is cushioned until birth. A child of human parents is *born out of water* (literal translation). A child of God is born of the Spirit. It seems that Jesus is saying something very simple: unless a person is born both physically and spiritually he cannot enter into the kingdom of God. This interpretation fits into the context, for Jesus goes on to say, "That which is born of the flesh is flesh; and that which is born of the Spirit is spirit."

   b. Ask *what two kingdoms Jesus speaks of in v. 5. How does one become a member* of the fleshly or human kingdom? How does one become a member of the kingdom of God?

Do not stop long on the subject of the new birth yet. It is the most important part of our study, but we will go right through the whole passage first, and then come back to it again.

   c. *In v. 7 Jesus says, "Marvel not." Why does He say this?*

   d. Ask the group for the *meaning of the illustration in v.* 8, and what it adds to the story. Add to their ideas any thoughts you received on the subject from your own study.

7. *Study v. 9.* Nicodemus still isn't satisfied with Jesus' answer. *Could the group state his next question in one word?* Nicodemus

is like so many of us: we think so much in terms of the physical kingdom that the spiritual kingdom is very unreal to us, and so we say we cannot understand it.

8. *Study vv.* 10-13.

a. *Even though Nicodemus did not understand* all about how the new birth takes place, *what did Jesus expect him to do* (see vv. 11b and 12)?

> "This is an illustration of what we were talking about in Romans 1. Nicodemus did not understand with his intellect all about the new birth, and therefore he did not want to receive as true what Jesus said, nor believe in Jesus as the only way into the kingdom of God. *He let his intellect come between him and God.* He would not believe in what he could not understand, and the last word we have from his lips in this story is, 'How?' He did not honor God as God, but became vain in his imaginations, refusing to accept anything that his intellect did not understand. Jesus' illustration of the wind was certainly appropriate in this case. In effect He said, 'You acknowledge the effects of the wind even though you do not understand its workings. But you do not receive the truths I tell you because you do not understand them fully '

> "Lots of us are like Nicodemus. When we are confronted with the necessity of regeneration, the new birth, we say, 'Well, I just don't understand how that can be. It's so illogical.' We want to understand it before we believe it. In other words, we trust our brain, and our thinking, more than God's Word. And God's reply to us is the same as it was for Nicodemus. Will you look again at v. 11? Jesus is in effect saying, 'I am

talking about something of which I *am absolutely sure,* something which I *know,* something which I *have seen;* and *you refuse* to accept my word, you don't believe me.' As long as we are in that condition God can do nothing for us. The Christian religion will require of us every bit of gray matter we have. It is not for lazy people who don't want to take the trouble to think. *But it can never be completely understood by the human intellect, and the man who waits to believe until he fully understands will never be born again.* Ultimately, the whole Christian religion is based on faith, and those of us who are to be born again must come to a place where we set aside our own ideas of God and our own thinking on the subject, and simply believe God's Word, not because we understand it fully, but *because it is God's Word.*"

b. *What was Jesus' authority for the emphatic statements He makes in vv. 3, 5, 7?* Nicodemus had said, "We know that thou art a teacher come from God." Jesus took him at his word and expected him to act upon it. If Nicodemus believed that Jesus was *from God,* he should have received what Jesus said (vv. 11-13).

The study can be broken into two parts at this point.

9. *Study v. 14.*

a. *Discuss the incident to which Jesus refers in v. 14a.* What was the people's sin? What was the remedy? What was God's part in the remedy? How did the people appropriate the remedy?

Moses was leading the people into a land which God had promised them, but the people doubted God's promise and complained bitterly that they would all be dead before they reached their destination.

They, like the people in Romans 1, did not honor God as God, but "became vain in their imaginations," and doubted God's Word. God provided a remedy, but the remedy did not automatically cure all the people. *Each person who had been bitten had personally to accept the remedy.* This was done by looking to the brass serpent. Those who looked showed that they believed God's Word that this was the remedy. The remedy involved forsaking their former sin of unbelief. Formerly they doubted; now they believed. *This was the only remedy God had.*

b. *Discuss the incident to which Jesus refers in v. 14b.* What is man's sin that made this remedy necessary? Is this the only remedy for sin? What was God's part in providing a cure for sin? What was Christ's part? What is our part in being cured?

The illustration of Numbers 21 can be applied in detail here. We have the same sin; God provided the remedy; Christ offered up Himself; we are cured by believing. The group should get all of these points on their own. Do not give help unless it is really necessary.

10. *Illustrate the difference between knowing and believing.* Ask the group to think of how they would explain to a friend the difference between *"knowing* that Jesus died for your sin," and *"believing* that Jesus died for your sin." Several illustrations have been used to make this clear. One that is frequently mentioned is that of a huge crowd of people watching the famous tight-rope walker, Blondin, cross the Niagara Falls in 1860. Blondin displayed his skill by crossing a number of times on a rope over 1,000 feet long and 160 feet above the water. The story is told that he then addressed the crowd, asking if they believed he could take one of them across. Of course, they all gave their assent. Then he asked someone to get on his back and go with him. The man who was invited

refused to go. When Blondin asked the man if he did not believe in his ability to take him across, the spectator assured him he did believe, but no amount of persuading or coaxing could induce him to get on Blondin's back and cross the Falls.

> "You know, that's just the way many people are. They want to remain *spectators* of Christianity. They are not willing to become *participants*. They know that Christ *can* save them from sin, but they *are not willing to believe Him,* to turn over their whole lives to Him. There is one point, incidentally, where this illustration does not apply. Going over the Falls on a rope involves taking a risk. *Believing in Christ involves no risk.* Jesus is able to save to the uttermost all those that come unto God by Him." (Cf. Hebrews 7:25.)

11. *Meditate on v. 16.* Use your own ideas in getting the group to think for a few minutes on the wonder of God giving His only Son to be the Saviour of the world.

CONCLUDE

Your conclusion today will be a little more lengthy than hitherto. Have the group concentrate again for a few minutes on the key verses of our study, *vv.* 5, 6, 7.

1. Referring to v. 5 ask them *what things begin for a person at natural birth that were not true before.* As the group names each of these things, take them one at a time and point out that when a person is born of the Spirit each of these things is true in the spiritual life. For example:

He is conscious—likewise he is conscious in the Spirit of spiritual things. *He can see*—likewise he can see in the Spirit. A whole new realm of life opens up to the new Christian that he did not know before existed. *He responds to people*—likewise he responds in the Spirit to God and others as he never did before.

He becomes a part of society—likewise in the Spirit he becomes a part of the society of God's children known as the church of God. Be careful not to take this illustration too far. Just make your points, and leave it at that.

2. *Have someone state again clearly and concisely the point made in v. 6.* Be sure it is made clear here that Jesus is really just stating a law that is very common to us in the natural world. Lots of the students will have read the life of Louis Pasteur, who proved that there was no such thing as spontaneous generation in the physical world.

> "Jesus is simply saying that it is the same in the spiritual realm. *There is no spontaneous generation.* Spiritual life in a person does not just suddenly form out of the atmosphere. *He must be born of God if he is to be a child of God.* This is a mystery. How it happens we cannot understand. But we know it is inevitably tied with our belief, our faith in God. Unless we believe in Christ who died for our sins, we cannot be born into God's family.
>
> "It is no wonder then that Jesus follows vv. 5 and 6 with v. 7: 'Ye must be born again.' *There is no other way.*"

3. Have the group answer this question to themselves, *"Have I been born again?"* Tell the group that we will be studying in the next two weeks more about Christ, and how we can enter God's kingdom. Make sure that anyone who wants to settle the matter immediately or who wants to ask more questions feels free to talk to someone in the group after the group study ends.

4. Close with one or two minutes of *silent prayer,* followed by having one of the students pray audibly.

six

WHAT DOES IT MEAN TO BELIEVE?

a leader's guide for group study of John 1:10-13

STUDY FIRST

May I remind you again! Do not read through this guide until you have done the study questions.

A. *Find out exactly what the passage says.*

1. Who (person or group) is spoken of in this passage?
2. List everything that is said about Christ.
3. List everything said about "the world."
4. List everything said about "his own."
5. List everything said about "all who received him."
6. List the ways in which a person does not become a son of God.
7. State the ways a person does become a son of God. What has Christ to do with it as stated in the text?

B. *Think about what the passage means.* This is the place for meditation. Don't just try to get an answer to each question, but think about each question for a while, and then jot down all the thoughts that came to you.

1. What do you think Christ's attitude would be toward the world which He had made, and in which He was living?

2. Consider Christ in relation to each of the three groups of people mentioned in the text.

a. It says, "The world knew him not." What does this mean? In what sense did they know Him? In what sense did they not know Him?

b. It says, "his own received him not." What does this mean? Why do you think they did not receive Him? How would you feel if you did not sense a welcome among those at school? How would you feel if you were unwanted by your parents, even though you lived in their house? How would you feel if the one whom you loved most ignored you? Christ loved "his own" more than any human being can love.

c. It speaks of "all who received him." Think for a while of what receiving Christ involves. Read as much as you can of John's Gospel, and see what you can find out about those who had a receptive attitude toward Christ, and those who did not.

Is it possible to accept Christ into your heart without giving Him your heart? Is it possible to accept Him as Saviour without accepting Him as Lord? Refer back to the first study on sin, especially Romans 1:21, before you decide about this. Is receiving Him just like receiving any gift which can be put away in a closet or drawer and forgotten once it has been received? Or is it more like receiving a person into your home, or perhaps like receiving a husband or wife as your life partner? Does receiving Christ involve any responsibility (Cf. v. 12)? (Some of these questions are repetitive or overlap. They are designed to guide your thinking about what it means to accept Christ.)

3. Meditate carefully on this next question. Why do you think the word "power" is used in v. 10? Why does it not just say "As many as received him . . . become sons of God"?

4. What is the point of v. 13? Compare it with John 3:6.

C. *Think about what the passage means to you,* i.e. what do each of the facts mean in relation to yourself?

1. Decide where you stand in relation to the three groups of people. That is,

   a. are you among those who know some of the surface facts about Christ, but who do not know the Christ as He really is, who do not know the real truth about His character and purpose in coming into the world? Or

   b. are you among those who know the real truth about Him and His purpose but have not received Him? Or

   c. are you among those who have received Him, and who are obeying Him?

2. **Decide** what you ought to do, depending upon which group you are in.

3. You have witnessed to a friend about God's plan of salvation so that he has seen his sin, wants to forsake it, understands the necessity of the new birth, and God's provision of the remedy for sin. He now wants to become a Christian. Imagine his saying to you, "I want to receive Christ. How do I do it?" What would be your answer? It is the responsibility of every Christian to have an answer for that question.

HAVE AN AIM

Your aim today should be to make clear that to receive Christ, or to believe in Christ for one's salvation, is not simply to say, "I believe that Jesus Christ died for my sins and I accept Him as my own personal Saviour." *Believing in Christ involves turning your life over to Him.* Instead of living a *self*-centered life you now live a *Christ*-centered life. This means that Christ is given His rightful place as Lord, and from then on the Christian's attitude to Christ is summed up in the prayer, *"Not my will, but Thine,* be done."

HAVE A METHOD OF PROCEDURE

Introduce the passage: "Today's study is, in a sense, the most important of this series. All the theory in the world about Christianity is of no use in witnessing unless one can tell a person *how* to accept Christ. Every Christian ought to be able to do this."

1. Have everyone get out pen and notebook and open their Bibles at John 1. Give them five minutes to read the passage (John 1:10-13), and answer the following questions: *Who (person or group) is spoken of in the text? List everything that is said about each.*

2. When the group is finished, *take up their answers.* When you have all the data before you, tell them that our study today will be centered around the meaning of the most important of these facts.

If there is a blackboard handy, you might list for their consideration something like that which is given below, listing the persons in the left-hand column, the facts in the right.

a. Christ:	In the world made the world came unto His own gave power
b. The world:	knew Him not
c. His own:	received Him not
d. All who received Him: All who believed Him:	given power to become sons of God

CONCENTRATE ON THE MAIN BODY OF TRUTH

1. Discuss the meaning of the facts about Christ.

a. "He was in the world." It would be well to call to the group's attention here the fact that *Jesus was not a recluse,* not an "armchair philosopher." He was in the world, not only in the sense that He was living on earth, but also in the sense that He lived right among the people. He gave people an opportunity to get to know Him.

> "Just the first four chapters of John show Jesus in a multitude of situations. He is found in five provinces, in four cities. He is doing His work by a river, on a roadside, in a home, in the temple, and by a well on a dusty road. He is contacting a great fellow-preacher, a keen young man, a group of happy people at a wedding reception, a church official, an immoral woman, a group subject to extreme racial prejudice, and a government official.
>
> "Jesus was 'in the world' in the truest sense of the word."

b. "The world was made by him." Perhaps to some members of the group the idea that *Christ was the agent of creation* will be a new idea. They might be interested in seeing another passage on the subject. Refer them to Hebrews 1:2c. If any problem is raised here about whether it was God or Christ who created the world, study the text from Hebrews carefully. You will see that God created the world *by Christ.* God initiated creation. Christ was the agent who carried out what God initiated.

Discuss how Christ would feel toward this world which He had made, and in which He now dwelt.

c. "He came unto his own." Who are His own? *Discuss how Christ would feel toward them.*

2. *Discuss the meaning of the fact about the world.*

a. "The world knew him not." Ask them what this fact means. *In what sense did the world know Christ? In what sense did it not know Him?*

After you have had several answers to the latter two questions, you might bring out here that the world knew Christ only in a superficial sense. They did not perceive His true character, they did not recognize who He was. They knew Him as a carpenter from Nazareth, as a man born in Bethlehem, as a lay preacher who went around preaching and talking with anyone who would listen, as a man who did miracles, fed His hungry followers, and incurred the wrath of religious officials. In a sense, they knew Christ; but they did not know the real Christ, the Son of God, the Saviour of the world. The world today is the same. It knows Christ as a good example, or as a great teacher, or perhaps as one of the greatest religionists the world has ever known. Many people think they know Christ, but they do not know the real Christ.

3. *Discuss the meaning of the fact about "his own."*

a. "His own received him not." For answers to the next two questions have the group draw on their general knowledge of the Gospels. *How was the unreceptive attitude of His own expressed? Was it all open hostility?* We have already studied four passages where an unreceptive attitude is illustrated. Try to get the group to think of these, as well as any others you may think of. Wherever possible, ask them questions rather than giving them the answers.

In Psalm 139 we mentioned the person who tries to wriggle out from under God's hand. It's like running out the back door when you see an unwanted friend ringing your doorbell. In Romans 1 we found people refused to recognize God, or His claims upon them. John 8 had in it the open hostility of the Pharisees who wanted to kill Jesus. Nicodemus too, in John 3, illustrates the unreceptivity of unbelief. He just didn't accept Jesus' word. These are just four pictures of the way people refused to receive Christ. If you had been Christ, how would you have felt?

There is a brief picture in the New Testament of how Christ did feel at being rejected by His own. I think it is one of the most heartbreaking of Christ's words. Read Matthew 23:37 aloud to the group. Is there any more comfortable sound than that of little chicks cheeping contentedly as they snuggle under their mother's wings? Jesus' one desire was to be a similar source of comfort and protection to His own, but He was denied that pleasure because *they would not.*

4. *Discuss the meaning of the facts about "all who received Him."*

a. *Have the group think about what it meant for the people in Jesus' day to receive Christ.* John's Gospel is full of two types of people: those who received and believed Christ, and those who did not receive Him. We have discussed the latter. Now have the group think about the receptive ones. How did they act toward Christ?

After the group has exhausted their ideas, your findings from the leader's study questions may be brought out here. In John 1:37 and following, there are two men who saw Jesus, followed Him, and spent the late afternoon and evening with Him. Apparently they had believed as much as they had been taught and had a heart-hunger for more, so they investigated more closely this new Teacher. *They wanted to be around Him* and learn. We do not know exactly when they were born again, but their first actions certainly show *they had a receptive attitude to the person of Christ* from the very outset. This is just one illustration. You can call the group's attention to others you found.

b. *Now try to give the group a better understanding of what it means to "receive" Christ, or to "believe in Him."* There is one idea that should be brought out clearly here. It is important because there seems to be some confusion in our thinking as to what it means to accept Christ.

> "We often hear Christ spoken of as a gift, to be received merely by saying to Him, 'I accept Thee as my Saviour, and want Thee to come into my heart,' or something of a similar nature. That is true; Christ is God's gift to man, and we have Him by merely accepting Him. But there is a sense in which this is not an adequate conception of what it means to accept Christ.

> "Let me illustrate. When I was a child, the superintendent of a Sunday school I was attending said one Sunday morning that he had a nickel in his hand for any child who would come up and receive it. No one came. After awhile I ventured up to the front, and he gave me the nickel. He then pointed out that Christ could be ours simply by accepting God's proffered gift, which was true. But there was one basic difference. When I received that nickel, I received a thing. When I received Christ, I received *a person. I could put the thing into my pocket and forget about it. I could not put the person into some remote corner of my life* and completely forget about Him. If I had done so, I would not really have accepted Him.

> "Think a bit about what it means in real life to accept *a person.* When *a friend* comes to visit you for a few days, if you receive that person with your heart as well as your hands, you will do everything possible to make that person feel at home and welcome. You will

not make him ask for anything he may need because you will be watching him closely, trying to anticipate his wishes, and to fulfill them before he can even voice them.

"It is similar with a *baby*. When parents accept a baby, they do not just accept all the joys and pleasures the baby can give them. They also accept the responsibilities. And unless they are prepared to accept the demands a baby will make upon their time, energy, affections, interests, and money, they ought not to have one. There may be times when the mother rebels inwardly against all that is demanded of her, but as her love for the baby grows, so does her willingness to sacrifice everything for her child if need be.

"There is another illustration which Christ Himself uses to clarify the relationship between Himself and His followers—*the marriage relationship*. Let us consider a few of the facts about marriage and compare them with our relationship to Christ.

"The church is spoken of frequently as the bride of Christ. When a girl marries she leaves her family and promises to take her husband from her wedding day forward, for better for worse, for richer for poorer, in sickness and in health, to *love, cherish,* and to *obey*. This is a tremendous vow to make *but she is not afraid to make that vow when she is sure of the person to whom she is making it.* Because she knows *him* she is not afraid to commit her whole self to him. But because this is such a serious step to take she does not do so without thinking it over carefully. Note the following quote from the marriage ceremony, 'Holy Matrimony is not by any to be enterprised, nor taken in hand, unadvisedly, lightly, or wantonly; but reverently, discreetly, advisedly, soberly, and in the fear of God.'

"With this context in mind consider some of Jesus' own words about discipleship. (Cf. Luke 14:25-33.)

"Some of you must be thinking, 'Does a person have to surrender completely his whole person to Christ if he is to accept Him? Can he not be my Saviour without being my Lord?' Let me ask you another question, if sin can be defined as refusing to let God be GOD, the Almighty, in your life, how can that sin be forgiven and cleansed away if you refuse to let Christ be Lord? Surely the whole point of man's redemption is that by it Christ takes His rightful place in our lives, by it His lordship is restored. By the second birth (John 3) man is given *a new heart which is glad to* restore Christ's lordship. A person who really accepts Christ as Saviour must have *a positive attitude toward Him,* a willingness to follow Him. The longer he lives with Christ the more demands Christ makes on his life. When such demands are made he may rebel against them. Although he loves Christ, he still loves himself, and it hurts to do what Christ asks. However, if he is a true Christian he will sooner or later yield to Christ's claims. He has *received Christ once and for all;* he must learn to *receive daily Christ's demands.*

"In summing up perhaps we could say that when a person receives Christ he may not be conscious of all the demands Christ will make upon his life, but *he must have no known reservations.*"

c. *Ask them why they think the word "power" is used in v.* 12. Why does it not just say "as many as received him become sons of God"?

As I was studying this question, I noticed that the marginal reading is "right or privilege." However, the new RSV still translates it "power." The thought came to me that Christ gives to those who receive Him power to become children of God in two senses. It is through His power that we become sons of God by birth. And it is also through His power that we become sons of God by life. Let me illustrate. I am my father's daughter by birth. But there is another sense in which I become more and more my father's daughter by the way I live. The more I make his standards, his ideals and ethics, his living faith, his personality, etc., a part of my own character, the more I become in reality his daughter. By daily practice I become in actuality what in theory I am by birth.

So it is with the one who has received Christ. He has to have Christ's power in order to be born into the family of God, but he also has to have Christ's power in order to live like a son or daughter of God. Christ gives power for both!

5. *Discuss what the facts mean to you.*

a. *Ask each person to decide* for himself quietly, without indicating his decision, *where he stands in relation to each of the three groups*: those who do not know Christ, those who have not received Christ, those who have received and believed.

b. Here might be a good place for a *few words from you,* if you are a Christian, as to *why you are glad you are a Christian.* You might simply say, if it is true, that you have received Christ as your Saviour and Lord. You would heartily recommend that anyone who is in the first two groups decide to receive Him. Do not prolong this, but *make it clear that you are "completely sold" on being a follower of Christ,* and that you do wish others could share your joy and peace. But, whatever you do, don't profess something you aren't experiencing! If what you say is not real, the group will know it.

c. Suggest that, when they get home, *those who have received Christ rethink their relationship to Him.* Are they personally committed to the person of Christ? Have they merely given mental assent to the fact that Jesus died for their sin, or *have they received a person into their lives "to love, cherish, and to obey"*?

d. Ask the group *what would be their reply if a person asked them this question, "How can I accept Christ as my Saviour?"*

Add anything you may have thought of. The main point here is that receiving Christ is a very simple thing. If you know you really want Him, it is simply a matter of *your choosing* to accept Him and all that He involves into your life. When you are a sinner, you want your own way; when you become a Christian you submit your will to Christ. You pray to God asking Him to forgive your sin against Him for Christ's sake, and asking Him to enter your life and take control of it. When you have done this, you know that He has done His part, and you thank Him for it.

CONCLUDE QUICKLY

If you believe there are people in the group who do not know Christ as Saviour, you might conclude simply by rereading the passage thoughtfully and slowly to the group, asking each one to pray silently that Christ may meet the present need in his life, whatever that might be. You might ask a mature Christian to close in prayer.

If there are only Christians present, you might challenge them with the fact that they have brought no non-Christians out. And close with a time of prayer, asking each person present to rededicate himself or herself to witnessing for Christ by lip and by life in school. What was said today about the meaning of receiving Christ is "strong meat" for some people. If you want further Scriptures on the subject the following will be found helpful: Luke 6:45; Matthew 7:21-29; John 3:36 in the ASV or RSV, Matthew 4:10; Romans 10:9 in the RSV; Ephesians 5:23, 24, 31, 32.

The following quote might help to clarify the issue too. It is taken from *The Way* by Robinson and Winward:

> "The word 'Christian' is used so vaguely and misused so widely nowadays, that it may be helpful to give a definition which is true to the teaching of our textbook, the New Testament. For having defined this word, the meaning of the phrase 'the Christian life' will then be clear.
>
> 'A CHRISTIAN IS A PERSON WHO HAS MET GOD IN CHRIST, AND WHO IS TRUSTING IN HIM AS SAVIOUR AND OBEYING HIM AS LORD.'
>
> "The Christian life is thus a personal relationship, resulting from a personal encounter between the Living Saviour and the human soul. No man can grow or develop into this life; there must be encounter, crisis, decision, acceptance, committal. The analogy of marriage used in the New Testament is illuminating; two people *meet* and are attracted. The man woos the girl, she accepts (or, of course, rejects) his proposal—in fact accepts him and gives herself to him, an acceptance which is sealed publicly in a covenant. Getting married is a definite act, and no man would dream of answering the question, 'Are you married?' by saying 'I'm not quite sure, but I hope so!' Likewise a Christian is a person who has responded to the initiative of the Saviour's redeeming love by a quite definite act of self-surrender, entering thereby into the 'new covenant.'"

seven

MAN'S EXTREMITY—GOD'S OPPORTUNITY

a leader's guide for group study of Hebrews 7:23-27

A WORD TO THE LEADER

Up to this point the study helps have been very long and detailed. Today's study is full of specific facts, most of which are well known. Instead of writing a lot about facts, I am simply going to ask a few questions. The leader should pray definitely to God that His Holy Spirit may take each fact and make it living and real. After you have studied on your own, line up your lesson plan and the questions you want to ask the group, using the study questions given below as a guide.

One of the most important things to learn in Bible study is the art of meditation, simply thinking about a fact until the fulness of that fact, *every detail* of it, has made its impact upon your heart and life. For example, the purpose of any of these study questions is not simply to get an answer to the question; it is to start your mind on a search for *all* the meaning of the fact. You can often give an answer to these questions without thinking. But there are quite a few of them that will require a lot of hard thinking if you are to give a full answer, if you are really to get at the "meat" of the Word.

Now turn to II Timothy 2:4-7. Note that in vv. 4, 5 and 6 Paul gives three illustrations: soldier, athlete, farmer. Now note what he says to young Timothy in v. 7. If Timothy, who had the privilege of being tutored under Paul, had to learn to *think for himself,* how much more do we!

Just one more word: *thinking is hard work.* At least I find it that way. It is no easy job to hit a big idea and grapple with it until you have mastered it—but it's so much more satisfying than taking the easy way out and going to a minister or someone else and asking him to explain the idea to you. Start now to try to solve your own problems, and do your own thinking with the help of the Holy Spirit, whom Jesus promises to guide us into all truth (John 16:13). It's a real challenge and I know you'll enjoy the thrill of achievement!

STUDY QUESTIONS

A. *Review the main teaching in each of the previous studies.*
Note that God's wrath is against the sinner in Romans 1, and we have not yet discussed how that wrath can be appeased. We have discussed the necessity of a rebirth, but have just touched on God's cure for sin in order to make the new birth possible. We are to study the cure for sin more fully today.

B. *Study the passage as a whole.*
   1. The whole book of Hebrews shows how Jesus, with the salvation He has purchased for us, is superior to the Old Testament system of sacrifice for sin. If you have time, therefore, read through the whole book of Hebrews, or more especially chapter 5:1-10 and chapters 7-10:8, in order to get a general background for 7:23-27.

If you are not familiar with the Old Testament system, read about it in Leviticus, chapters 1-10.

2. Reread 7:23-27. To whom does the "they" in v. 23 refer? After you have read the passage thoughtfully several times, decide what the subject of it is, and state the subject in a few words.

C. *Study the passage verse by verse.*

1. Divide a page of your notebook in half vertically. Put the heading "Christ" at the top of one side, and "Levitical Priests" at the top of the other. Now go through the passage verse by verse, listing everything that is said about each. You should get a total of about sixteen facts. From your knowledge of Scripture, and your reading of other parts of the book of Hebrews, fill in any facts about the Levitical priesthood which are not definitely stated but which are implied in the contrast. For example, it says that Christ offered up Himself, and we know from other Scriptures that the priest offered up animals and birds.

2. Label each fact as to whether it refers to the character or to the work of the Levitical priests and Christ.

3. Consider the contrast between Christ's character and the other priests'. Why is each fact important? What difference would it make to you if Christ had not had each of the characteristics you noted?

4. Note especially Christ's character in v. 26. The word "harmless" could better be translated "blameless." See if you can determine the different shades of meaning given in these four characteristics. In other words, is the author just repeating himself or is there a difference between holy and blameless, between holy and undefiled, etc.?

5. Consider the contrast between Christ's work and the priests'. What difference does it make to you in terms of money, time, effort, peace of mind, consciousness of sin, etc., that Christ's sacrifice was *Himself,* and that He was offered *once for all?* What

difference does it make to you in terms of a sense of guilt, your access to God's throne, Christian living, etc., that Christ is continually interceding before God on your behalf on the basis of that sacrifice?

6. What does "to the uttermost" mean to you? What are the things in your life for which you need an "uttermost" salvation, the things in your character and personality of which you are ashamed, the habits which you cannot break, the resolutions which are never fulfilled? Is God able to care for these things? Note the marginal reading of the word. Are you encouraged when you realize that all the days ahead of you are taken care of by the word "evermore"?

D. *Review the passage as a whole (re-view or take another look at it).*

1. V. 26 says, "Such an high priest became us." Or, as someone has put it, *"He was exactly what we needed."* Write two paragraphs on this idea: one on the adequacy of Christ's character, and one on the adequacy of Christ's work in dealing with sin in your life.

2. If you are really serious about going on with the Lord, take time to memorize what you think is the key verse of this passage.

3. There are several hymns on the subject of Christ's death and intercession for us which are an inspiration to read or sing. You might want to make use of one or several of the following in your group study. You might have someone sing a solo at the close of the meeting while the group listens prayerfully.

(In IVCF *Hymns* are "O Christ, What Burdens Bowed Thy Head," p. 126; "The Veil is Rent! Lo, Jesus Stands," p. 128; and "Arise, My Soul Arise," p. 109.)

Note: There are other aspects of Christ's atonement which have not been touched on here. The following are a few of the many passages on this subject which could be studied to your profit if you wish to take the time: Isaiah 53; Ephesians 2:8-18; Romans 5:6-11; Romans 3:21-26.

eight

WHERE DO WE GO FROM HERE?

a leader's guide for group study of Colossians 2:6, 7

STUDY FIRST

A. Before you open your Bible, imagine that you are compiling a dictionary. Write out definitions for the following words: receive, walk, root, build, establish, faith, abound and thanksgiving. Then look them up in a standard dictionary and add any shade of meaning which you may have omitted.

Now rewrite Colossians 2:6, 7 using your definition in place of each word. Do not try to apply it particularly to the Christian life, but just rewrite the passage using the definition.

B. Meditate on the spiritual meaning of each word you defined. One or two questions are given below concerning each word. They will help to start you thinking, but do not stop there. Get some ideas of your own.

1. How does one receive Christ? Therefore how ought one to walk? Why is it impossible to walk any other way?

2. Why does it say "walk" rather than "run" or "fly"?

3. To what part of your spiritual life could a "root" be likened? What does one's spiritual root absorb? What food does it store? What soil is it rooted in?

4. Does it require any effort on the Christian's part to be "built up in Him"? Are there any prefabricated buildings in God's kingdom?

5. How does one become established? An establishment has to have a firm foundation or basis. What is this foundation for the Christian?

6. How do you think "the faith" is?

7. Why is it important to "abound in thanksgiving"? Is thanksgiving an attitude or a definite, deliberate act? Can it be governed by the will?

C. Having found out what the passage says, and what it means, think about what it means to you. *Before you look at the following questions,* meditate on the passage, jotting down anything that strikes you as applying directly to your life.

1. Have you been "walking" in the same way as you "received" Christ? Why is it impossible to walk any other way? If you have been trying to walk in your own strength, what ought you to do about it?

2. Is your life too heavy; that is, does the building overbalance the roots? If so, how can you rectify the situation?

3. In what specific way is it necessary for you to be established in the faith?

4. Are you abounding in thanksgiving? If you are not thankful, how can you become so?

HAVE AN AIM

Aim to stress today that Christ is received by *faith*, and that it is only *by faith* that we can walk in Him. Accepting Christ by faith,

75

and then attempting to live for Him in your own strength is only doomed to failure. When we received Him, we received power by faith to be born of God. When we walk in Him, we receive power by faith to be all that this verse describes: rooted, built up, established, and abounding in thanksgiving.

HAVE A METHOD OF PROCEDURE

Introduce the study. I think that I would not give any introduction which would indicate the subject matter of today's study. Simply have the students take out notebook and pen and write definitions for the words in Colossians 2:6, 7. Divide up the words so that each student writes only one or two definitions, and ask them to define as if they were writing a dictionary.

CONCENTRATE ON THE MAIN BODY OF TRUTH

1. When the group is finished writing their definitions, have them work together on rewriting Colossians 2:6, 7, using their own definitions and anything which you found in your study that would be helpful. By the time they have finished this, they will have a pretty good understanding of what the passage says.

If you have never before tried rewriting a passage in this way, do it with other passages in your own Bible study every once in a while. It often opens up new truths to you. In case the idea is new to you, and you don't quite get what I mean, a rewriting of Colossians 2:6, 7 is given below. It was done by using Webster's dictionary definitions.

> "As you therefore have permitted Christ Jesus the Lord to enter into your life, so advance step by step in Him. There should be a part of your spiritual life which is not noted for its beauty, and which does not produce other Christians, but which is the growing center of your life. Its function is to absorb food from the Bible,

to breathe air in prayer, to store food for necessary spiritual reserves, and to act as a necessary means of support when your spiritual life is attacked by prevailing winds. This part of you is the *root* of your soul. Through Christ's resources, you should also have a part of you which is seen. This building should be set on a firm basis, the basis of your complete confidence in God. Having all this, your life should teem with your prayers of gratitude to God."

Do not read the above paraphrase to the group, or if you do wish to read it, don't do so until after you have done the next section with them. It is really given only as a little help for the leader, and incidentally, is not to be considered sound exegesis.

2. Now *discuss with the group what the passage means.* Use as a basis for your discussion the questions found in question B. of the leader's assignment. Add to these any questions of your own that will help them to see what you have found in the passage.

3. Use the questions under letter C. in the leader's assignment as a basis for discussing what the *passage means to them personally.* Some of these questions are quite personal, and the students may prefer to write their answers rather than say them. Give them plenty of time to think over the answers. Nothing will be gained by posing the questions quickly, one after the other.

4. When the students have finished writing, *ask them to share with the group anything that they have received from today's study,* anything that they wish to change or remedy in their lives, or anything they wish to improve upon. If no one offers to speak up, you might ask several of the Christians who really seem to be growing in their Christian lives *to tell some of the lessons they have learned, or the things which they have found most helpful in their walk with God.* For example, being "rooted in Him" is closely

related to the *Quiet Time.* They might tell about some method of Bible study, or of keeping a prayer list, or about some method of Scripture memorization which they have found helpful. Then, being "built up in Him" can relate to the outer *part of your Christian life which people see.* Someone might tell of how God has helped to gain better control of a bad temper, or a gossipy tongue, or of how he has been helped to be less selfish, etc. If you do not have people in your group who are ready for this type of witnessing on the spur of the moment, you might ask several ahead of time to be prepared to contribute something along one of the lines mentioned above. This would also be a good place for you to give the group some of the things which *you* have found a help in living the Christian life. Maybe your remarks will help someone else to share their experiences.

CONCLUDE QUICKLY
I think it would be a good idea to close today's study by re-emphasizing the first verse of the study. Point out again that we received Christ *through faith* in His power to save us, and that we can hope to walk the Christian life only *through faith* in Him.

Note: For other studies on the Christian life you might refer to Matthew, chapters 5 to 7; Romans 12; I Corinthians 13; Philippians 2:1-16; Ephesians 6:1-20.

nine

WHAT FUTURE IS THERE IN IT?

a leader's guide for group study of Acts 1:6-11

STUDY FIRST

1. Read the passage thoughtfully then give it a title of just two or three words that recalls to your mind the main thought or thoughts.

2. Who are the "they" of v. 6? Who is the "him" of v. 6? What had happened to "him" during the six weeks prior to the incidents we are studying today? (Cf. Acts 1:1-5.)

In vv. 3 to 5 the author, Luke, gives a brief review of a thrilling story which he had written in detail to Theophilus at an earlier date. If you have time, turn to "the former treatise," that is, the Gospel according to Luke, and read the closing chapters, 22 to 24. Try to imagine that you were one of His disciples, and that you went through those awful and wonderful days with Him. It will take you only about fifteen minutes to do this, and by it you will gain a grand background for today's study. Read from the RSV New Testament if possible.

BASIC CHRISTIANITY

3. Look at vv. 6 to 8. Here we find the risen Christ talking with the disciples. Note then that in v. 9 Jesus is the ascended Christ, and in vv. 10 and 11 He is the coming Christ. As you study this passage, think of it as centering around Christ, the LIVING Christ: *risen, ascended, and coming*.

4. *Study vv. 6-8.*

   a. What do you think prompted the question in v. 6?

   b. State Jesus' answer to their question in your own words. There are certain things in God's plan of salvation which are His responsibility, and His alone. There are other things which are our responsibility. Jesus makes this very clear here: what is God's business, and what is ours? Should Christians spend a lot of time trying to figure out when Christ is going to return and set up His kingdom? If not, why not? If not, what should we spend our time doing?

   c. Two facts are stated in v. 8. Note the order in which they are stated. Why do you think they are in this order?

   d. To what is the Christian to be a witness?

   e. Draw a rough map of the Mediterranean area, and locate on it Jerusalem, Judaea, and Samaria. Color Judaea and Samaria red. Look at the huge white area that would have been left in darkness if the disciples had not gone outside Jerusalem, or outside Judaea and Samaria in their witness. Note the attitude of most Jews toward Samaria. (Cf. John 4:9.)

   f. Draw a map of the world, and locate on it what you would consider your Jerusalem, your Judaea, and your Samaria. Color these areas in red. Are you witnessing now in your Jerusalem? Jesus said that is the place to begin. What are you planning to do about witnessing in Judaea and Samaria? Now look at what you have colored in and look at the large areas that might be considered the end of the earth. Are you planning to do anything about this area? If so, what?

g. Obeying Christ's commission is a big job. What difference does it make to you that the One who puts this heavy responsibility upon you is the *risen Christ?*

5. *Study v. 9.*

a. How do you think the disciples felt at seeing the *risen Christ* disappear? Can you recall from one of the other studies what work the ascended Christ is doing now? (Cf. Hebrews 7:25.) How can the ascended Christ help you in accomplishing the job He has given you to do?

6. *Study vv. 10, 11.*

a. What facts would you know about Christ's second coming if you had only v. 11 upon which to base your belief? What would the rest of the passage (vv. 6 to 10) add? How could meditation upon the fact of the *coming* Christ help you in your witness for Him from day to day?

7. Probably you won't have time to do this now, but some time read right through the Book of Acts at one sitting, and note what the risen Christ, the ascended Christ, and the coming Christ meant to the disciples. How did *He* help them to fulfill His command to be witnesses in Jerusalem, Judaea, Samaria, and the uttermost part of the earth?

HAVE AN AIM
Your study today should make clear that Christ's desire for us is not that we should worry about when He will return, but that we should be busy at the job He has given us to do until He does return. This job can be done alone through Him, the living Lord Jesus Christ.

The *risen* Christ gives us *power* for our work.

The *ascended* Christ gives us *confidence* before God.

The *coming* Christ gives us the *courage* to face any difficulties for Him.

HAVE A METHOD OF PROCEDURE

Introduce the study. You might begin by asking the group whether anyone has ever heard the last words of a dying man or woman. They need not answer this question vocally, but have them think with you about a person's last words on this earth. You may bring out the fact that when a person is about to leave this world, he says that which he considers most important. He wants to leave with his friends and loved ones the best of what life has taught him. A person's last words are not to be considered lightly.

> "Today we are to study the last words on earth of the most important Person who ever lived. And it is interesting that His last words have to do with a subject that most people are vitally concerned about. Let us open our Bibles and see what Jesus said the last time He saw His disciples on earth. You will find this last conversation in Acts 1:6-11."

CONCENTRATE ON THE MAIN BODY OF TRUTH

1. *Give the group two or three minutes to read through the passage.* Have them begin with v. 1 so that they will get a bit of the background for vv. 6 to 11.

2. *Who are the "they" of v. 6? Who is the "him" of v. 6?* If you did question 2 of the leader's study you will be able to give the group a little sketch of what Christ and the disciples had gone through during the six weeks prior to today's lesson. Do not take more than a few minutes for this.

3. *Have the group look at vv. 6 to 8, and point out that here*

we find the *risen* Christ. Have them note Jesus as the *ascended* Christ in v. 9, and the *coming* Christ promised in vv. 10 and 11.

"As we study this passage, let us think of it as centering around Christ, the *living* Christ: risen, ascended, coming."

4. *Study vv. 6-8.*

a. *What does the group think prompted the question in v. 6?* People today are just as eager and anxious as the disciples were. They want to know when Christ will come again.

b. *Have them state Jesus' answer to the disciples' question in their own words.* There are certain things in God's plan of salvation which are His responsibility, and His alone. There are other things which are our responsibility. Jesus makes this very clear here. *What is God's business? What is our responsibility?*

c. *Should Christians spend a lot of time trying to figure out when Christ is going to return and set up His kingdom?* This question cannot be answered dogmatically Yes or No because Christ wanted His followers to be discerning. (Cf. Matthew 24:32, 33.) But note also that His main emphasis is that no man knows exactly when Christ is returning, and our main job is to be witnesses to Him in the meantime. We are to "occupy" until He comes. (Cf. Matthew 25:27, and Luke 19:13.) When our concern over the time of Christ's return interferes with our active work for enlarging Christ's kingdom, we are not doing what Christ would have us do.

d. There are *two facts stated* in v. 8. Note the order in which they are stated. *Why do you think they are in this order?* It should be noted here that the Christian cannot possibly be a witness to Christ apart from the power of the Holy Spirit. The Christian's job is to tell what Christ has done for Him and for all men, but unless the Holy Spirit enables him, his words will be empty and without effect. A car is made as a means of transportation, but it cannot run without gasoline. No more can we run the Christian race without the Holy Spirit.

e. *To what is the Christian to be a witness?* The group will very readily answer, "to Christ," and may wonder why you asked such an obvious question. But have the students stop and think for a minute about their own witnessing. To what do they witness? Some will find that they witness to the fact that a Christian does not do certain things. This is not witnessing to *Christ*. Some witness to the value of going to a good evangelical church. Some witness to the value of reading one's Bible. These things are all good in·their place, but are not *in themselves* a witness *to Christ*. The disciples concentrated their verbal witness on Christ, *who He was,* and *what He did.* This was the center of their message.

f. If you have a blackboard, *draw a rough sketch of the Mediterranean area* on it, and point out Jerusalem, Judaea and Samaria to the group. If you don't have a board just point out with your hands the relative positions of the three places mentioned.

g. *Now have the group consider the area in which they live,* and decide what might be their Jerusalem, their Judaea, and their Samaria. Ask them what they are doing about each area, and what their responsibility is toward the end of the earth. Point out that whether or not we go to the end of the earth to witness, it is still our responsibility to see that it is reached through our prayers and our gifts.

h. Ask the group *what difference it makes to them that the One who puts the heavy responsibility of witnessing upon their shoulders is the risen Christ?* One cannot, in a brief paragraph, exhaust all the blessings that come to us through the resurrection of Christ. But there is one thing that seems to be connected with this passage, and I feel it should be brought out here.

"When Christ was about to leave the earth He promised the disciples that when He left He would send the Holy

BASIC CHRISTIANITY

Spirit to be their help. (Cf. John 16:7.) The Holy
Spirit gives us power to live like Christ and power
to do His work. (Cf. Acts 1:8.) But this power was
made available to us through Christ's resurrection. (Cf.
Ephesians 1:19, 20.) Because Christ had the power to
overcome death, we may have that power to live 'over-
coming' lives. We can be victors through the *risen*
Christ. How often we sing, 'I serve a risen Saviour,'
and yet how seldom we really claim the power that
the risen Saviour released for us!"

5. *Study v. 9.*

a. *How do they think the disciples felt at seeing their
risen Christ disappear?*

b. Can they recall from one of the other studies *what
work the ascended Christ is now doing* (Hebrews 7:25)? Ask them
how the ascended Christ can help in accomplishing the job He
has given them to do. If you do not get any answers, you might
give your own answer to this question. If you want to make the
question more specific, you might ask,

"When you make a flop of things, and feel as if you
have not done what God wants you to do, how does
it help to know that Christ is interceding for you?"

"When you sin and are ashamed to face God again, does
it help to know that the ascended Christ is interceding
for you before God because He has once and for all
paid the penalty for your sins?"

6. *Study vv. 10, 11.*

a. *What does v. 11 teach about Christ's second coming?*
What does the rest of the passage add?
The following should be made clear:

(1) Christ's coming is an absolute *certainty.*

(2) The *same Jesus* who went up will return.
(3) He will come in the *same way* He went.
(4) The time of His return is not for us to know.
(5) The Father has *fixed the time* for Christ's return (see RSV).

b. *How could meditation upon the fact of the coming Christ help us in our witness for Him?* It might be well to bring to the group's attention that witnessing for Christ does not only involve the lip (what one says), but the life as well (what one is and does). Perhaps the greatest help the thought of the second coming gives us is *encouragement.*

"Do you ever feel that there is no use in trying any more, that non-Christians have the best deal, that your witness isn't noticed, and everything seems pretty futile? Well, it may not happen often, but when discouragement does strike, just turn your thoughts to the *coming* Christ. He is coming to establish justice and righteousness; your labors will be rewarded then if they are not appreciated now. And then you won't be defeated by sin any more. You will be able to worship and serve Christ perfectly. Therefore encourage one another with these words in I Thessalonians 4:16-18; 5:11. Because Christ is coming your labor for Him is never in vain (I Corinthians 15:54-58)."

CONCLUDE THE STUDY

"Just before we close our study today, let us go back to the time of Christ and see what difference the risen, ascended, and coming Christ made in the lives of the Apostles.

"When Jesus was crucified, He left a pretty poor bunch

of disciples behind Him: a quarrelsome, frightened, selfish group—no worse than we would have been under the circumstances, but *no better* either. If you will read the Book of Acts, with the character of the Disciples in mind, you will find them entirely different. In fact you would not recognize them as the same people: they are now co-operative, courageous, Christ-centered warriors. They stormed the pagan world of their day, and turned it into a stronghold for God. What made the difference?

"For an answer to that question, let us look at just two incidents in the Book of Acts: one a story of murder, and the other of imprisonment and cruelty."

1. *Tell the group how Stephen was preaching about Christ,* and his listeners didn't like what he had to say. Then read Acts 7:54-60.

    a. "What gave Stephen the courage to die victoriously (v. 56)?"

    b. "If the *ascended* Christ can give such help at the time of death, will He not be sufficient for *all* of our problems?"

2. *Now take the group to the story of Paul's imprisonment* with Silas in Philippi. Read Acts 16:22-25.

"If you were sitting in a dark, dirty prison with your feet in stocks, and your back bleeding, would you sing? What power made Paul treat his afflictions in this way? What gave him such perseverance? Was it not the power of Christ's resurrection, and the encouragement of Christ's certain coming?

"About ten years after Paul had this experience, he wrote a letter to the church which was founded as a result of his sufferings and labor. As far as is known,

the church at Philippi was the purest and most faithful
of all the New Testament churches."

Have the group turn to this letter and note two things which Paul
says that give us a clue to the source of his Christian endurance.

    a. Have them note Paul's reference to the *power* of Christ's
resurrection (Philippians 3:10).

    b. Call their attention to the sure hope Paul had in Christ's
return (Philippians 3:20, 21).

"Surely the living Christ, risen, ascended, coming, can
make of us witnesses worthy of His Name."

In closing you may read slowly and meaningfully the following
hymn:

> *I know that my Redeemer lives:*
>   *What comfort this sweet sentence gives!*
> *He lives, He lives, who once was dead*
>   *He lives, my everlasting Head.*
>
> *He lives, triumphant from the grave;*
>   *He lives, eternally to save;*
> *He lives, all-glorious in the sky;*
>   *He lives, exalted there on high.*
>
> *He lives, to bless me with His love,*
>   *And still He pleads for me above;*
> *He lives to raise me from the grave,*
>   *And me eternally to save.*
>
> *He lives, my kind, wise, constant Friend;*
>   *Who still will keep me to the end;*
> *He lives, and while He lives I'll sing,*
>   *Jesus, my Prophet, Priest, and King.*
>
> *He lives my mansion to prepare;*
>   *And He will bring me safely there;*
> *He lives, all glory to His name!*
>   *Jesus, unchangeably the same!*
>   **S. MEDLEY.**